Unique
Process
Advisors

Printed in Toronto, Canada. May 2008. The Strategic Coach Inc., 33 Fraser Avenue, Suite 201, Toronto, Ontario, M6K 3J9.

This publication is meant to strengthen your common sense, not to substitute for it. It is also not a substitute for the advice of your doctor, lawyer, accountant, or any of your advisors, personal or professional.

Library and Archives Canada Cataloguing in Publication

Sullivan, Dan, 1944-
    Unique process advisors / Dan Sullivan.

ISBN 978-1-897239-15-5

    1. Financial services industry.   2. Investment advisors.   3. Financial planners.   I. Title.

HG179.5.S86 2008   332.6   C2008-903210-1

Contents

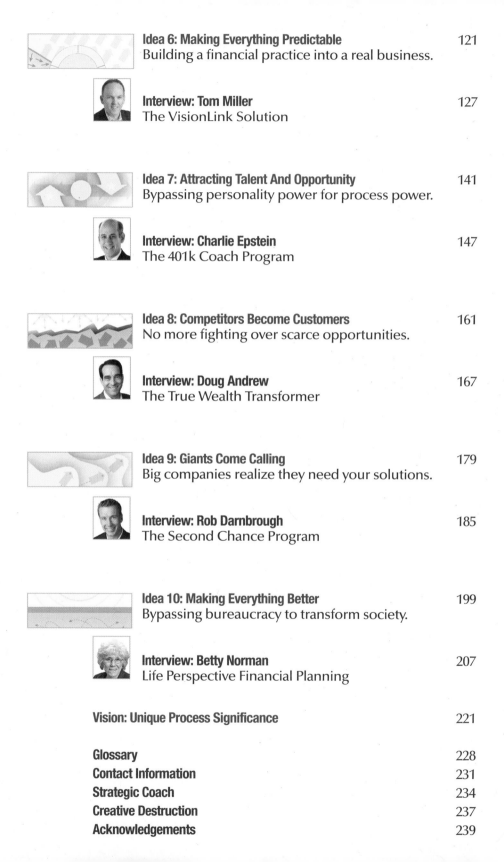

MODEL

The Unique
Process
Structure

Advisors with Unique Processes have already shown themselves to be dramatically more valuable and successful. This Unique Process approach becomes the blueprint for developing and expanding a truly entrepreneurial business and career.

The Unique Process Structure

Vehicle of independence for creative advisors.

The last 20 years have seen two important and opposing changes in the status of financial advisors. On one hand, the majority of advisors have lost much of their entrepreneurial freedom, becoming circumscribed and controlled by bureaucratic and regulatory constraints.

On the other hand, a powerful minority of advisors have become more independent, creative, and valuable in the marketplace. This book is about some of the most creative of the independent advisors, and about the unique approach they are using to create transformations for their clientele and freedom for themselves.

This approach is called the "Unique Process," and in this book I provide ten examples of how Unique Process™ Advisors have dramatically changed their financial businesses and careers.

A declaration of independence for creative advisors.
The structure of the Unique Process™ offers a decisively new, different, and better way to operate in the 21st century marketplace. Advisors with Unique Processes have already shown themselves to be dramatically more valuable and successful. The Unique Process approach becomes the blueprint for developing and expanding a truly entrepreneurial business and career. An entirely new and influential advisor community is already assembling and growing around this entrepreneurial model. The most advanced financial advisors in this

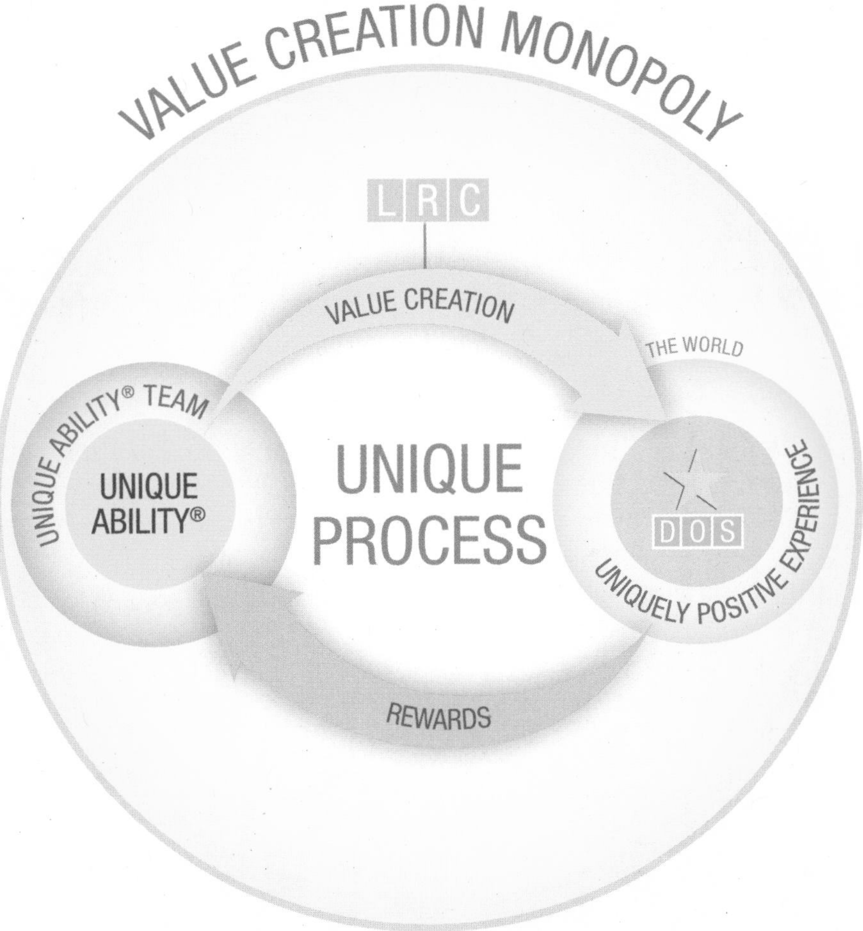

VALUE CREATION MONOPOLY

L R C

VALUE CREATION

THE WORLD

UNIQUE ABILITY® TEAM

UNIQUE
ABILITY®

UNIQUE
PROCESS

D O S

UNIQUELY POSITIVE EXPERIENCE

REWARDS

Unique Process community have developed their business models as participants in the Strategic Coach® Program, where they continually share their insights and innovations with hundreds of other entrepreneurs who are developing Unique Process businesses in dozens of other industries.

As it relates to the financial services industry, the success and impact of this influential community around a common, evolutionary structure is a declaration of independence for skillful, creative, client-focused advisors.

The structure of a Unique Process for financial advisors.
The structure of a Unique Process starts with two unique components: the Unique Ability* of the financial advisor, and the unique D.O.S.* issues of an individual financial services client in the marketplace.

1. The advisor's Unique Ability®: Financial advisors have traditionally received similar training in the industry. However, they vary enormously in the innate attitudes and skills with which they utilize this training. These innate factors are what we call Unique Ability®, which, when integrated and focused, has four crucial characteristics: *a superior skill that is widely recognized; a source of daily passion for the advisor; energizing for both the advisor and everyone who works with them; and a source of never-ending improvement.* In short, Unique Ability® is the "sweet spot" of every advisor's daily activity. To the degree that an advisor can operate within a circle of activities having these four characteristics, they are always energized and energizing, and productive and impactful in their work.

2. The clients' D.O.S.™ issues: At the corporate level, the financial services industry looks at financial consumers through the lens of the products and services these consumers can be encouraged to purchase. But the consumers see their lives very differently. *Their daily concerns are with their "D.O.S.*

issues": the dangers to their security, success, and status that cause them to be anxious, worried, or fearful; the opportunities for personal and professional progress that give them a sense of excitement and urgency; and the existing strengths that give them a sense of confidence, well-being, and peace of mind.

The key to being a uniquely valuable financial advisor, then, lies in being able to use your Unique Ability® to help financial clients and customers do three things: eliminate their dangers, capture their opportunities, and maximize their strengths—and continue to do this on an ongoing basis, so clients feel that their lives are being transformed.

3. Value creation: Financial advisors who are clear about both their own Unique Ability® and the D.O.S. issues of their clientele are in a position to create value in ways that are uniquely different. This value creation comes from providing three types of "uniquely positive" experiences that financial clients and customers in today's marketplace crave. *We refer to these three experiences as "L.R.C.," which stands for leadership, relationship, and creativity. Because of the bewildering array of financial dangers and resources in today's world, people can become confused, lose confidence, and find themselves without the capabilities necessary to make good decisions and take effective action.* Advisors who combine their Unique Ability and understanding of D.O.S. provide leadership, relationship, and creativity in forms that are uniquely different from the majority of financial advisors, who are only attempting to sell products.

4. Unique Experience: The clients who receive the benefit of this uniquely packaged L.R.C. feel that their situation is being transformed in uniquely positive ways. This "Unique Experience" becomes the basis of intense client commitment and loyalty toward the advisor. Clients feel that this custom-designed service is crucial to their future and that they can't get it anywhere else at any price.

5. Rewards: Advisors who are able to provide this kind of Unique Experience are extraordinarily well rewarded. *These rewards take the form of extra fees, much larger commissions, repeat and expanded business, and a constant flow of the best referrals.* The advisors' revenues and profits continually grow within this value-based relationship.

6. Unique Ability® Team: As advisors' businesses continually grow in profitability, increased surpluses are used to build a skilled team of specialists who further free up the time and attention of advisors to focus on their Unique Ability, and on deepening their understanding of clients' D.O.S. issues.

7. Unique Process: The constant repetition of this cycle of deepening Unique Ability®, greater mastery of D.O.S., increasing L.R.C. value creation, more positive Unique Experiences, and higher rewards leads to the formation of a Unique Process at the center. This process is a formalized structure and methodology that, once identified and packaged, becomes a means for continually improving every aspect of the value creation cycle.

8. Value Creation Monopoly: The formalization of the Unique Process now differentiates these advisors from all competition in the marketplace. A growing number of clients now see themselves as the special recipients of an extraordinary value creation methodology that is irreplaceable. The Unique Process Advisors are now in a position to escape from the bureaucratic and regulatory restrictions of a commoditized financial industry. In doing so, they become Industry Transformers*—role models for thousands of other advisors.

      *For the definition of Industry Transformer, please see page 229.

STORY

Unique Process Pioneers

The successes of these Unique Process Advisors, all using a common organizational structure, are important for many reasons. Perhaps the most important is that their examples lay out a practical plan and path for thousands of advisors to follow with equally valuable and satisfying results.

Unique Process Pioneers

Value creation for 21st-century clientele.

This is the story of how ten financial advisors operating in today's marketplace have transformed their businesses to attain higher levels of productivity, profitability, and impact. In doing so, they are pioneering a new way that business can done by many other advisors. In each case, the means for transformation was the Unique Process model described in the previous section. The successes of these Unique Process Advisors, all using a common organizational structure, are important for many reasons. Perhaps the most important is that their examples lay out a practical plan and path for thousands of advisors to follow with equally valuable and satisfying results.

Great progress. It is my hope and intention in writing this book that it will become a continual source of inspiration and direction to thousands of financial advisors, and will help transform their businesses in similar ways to our ten featured advisors. My hopes in this regard are well-founded, as you will read, because these ten Unique Process Advisors and hundreds of others in the Strategic Coach Program are already making great progress.

The transformative story that follows is told in two ways: through the firsthand accounts of the ten advisors, and through the identification of ten differentiating ideas that have emerged from their combined initiatives and achievements. Here's a brief synopsis of whom you'll be meeting in the pages ahead:

• **Dan Taylor:** *The Parent Care Solution*™
Having undergone a difficult period of caring for his own eld-
erly father, Dan Taylor, from Charlotte, North Carolina, transformed his experiences and insights into *The Parent Care
Solution.* This comprehensive approach enables other adult
children of aging parents to design intelligent and compas-
sionate gameplans for dealing with all the issues related to an
increasingly common experience for millions of people in
today's society. *The Parent Care Solution* enables Dan, as an
advisor, to focus on the crucial issues related to estate planning, medical and institutional care, legal documentation, and
the provision for legacies—all within a single process.

Packaging extraordinary solutions. Dan Taylor is a superb
example of an intelligent and skillful financial advisor who has
been able to "package" his unique wisdom from over 20 years
of experience with thousands of clients. As a coach to over
6,000 financial advisors since the 1970s, I've encountered many
advisors like Dan who have unique insights and have created
extraordinary solutions for their clientele. By having a Unique
Process, these advisors are able to capture and utilize an entire
career's worth of knowledge and problem-solving capabilities,
and combine them into a unified approach.

• **Mary Anne Ehlert:** *The Process For Protected Tomorrows*™
Mary Anne, because of her personal and professional experiences, had developed great insight into how the families of individuals with special needs could be helped by a combination of
counseling, facilitation, and financial planning. Mary Anne packaged this overall insight into *The Process For Protected
Tomorrows,* which provides a one-stop solution to helping these
families for the entire lifetime of the person with special needs.

Everything starts with the client. Mary Anne's process has now
become a major solution to a difficult situation that affects

over 54 million people in the United States. She now has all the major institutions and professions that deal with families with special needs coming to her for a unified and practical approach that makes their work more effective and efficient. Mary Anne has succeeded where thousands of experts and other advisors have failed because, in *The Process For Protected Tomorrows*, everything is designed with the specific welfare of the person with special needs and their family at the center. The sale of financial products is something that comes at the very end, and is of secondary importance.

• **Lee Brower:** *The Empowered Wealth System*™
Lee, from Bountiful, Utah, works with another very specific group of clients: wealthy families who have experienced the dispiriting and damaging consequences of having an over-abundance of financial resources but a deficiency of family purpose. Lee's *Empowered Wealth System* brings about a deep and lasting integration of each family's resources and capabilities, enabling it to become a powerful force for social improvement and progress.

Transforming direction, confidence, and capability. All Unique Process Advisors have discovered something powerful in the course of developing their Unique Processes: *that what clients most want today are transformative conversations, not commoditized products.* "Transformative" means in-depth conversations that identify, clarify, and utilize clients' most important issues in the present and the greatest aspirations for the future. This kind of conversation transforms the sense of direction, confidence, and capability of all who take part in it. This includes the Unique Process Advisors themselves, who find that by enabling their clients to design powerful futures, they differentiate themselves powerfully, positively, and permanently from other advisors in the financial marketplace.

- **Scott Keffer:** *The Donor Motivation Program*™
Scott, from Pittsburgh, focuses his transformative conversations on the area of philanthropic giving in America and Canada. His *Donor Motivation Program* enables all parties involved in charitable gifting—charities, donors, and financial advisors—to develop extraordinarily successful and satisfying teamwork within a single integrative process that can be utilized in any area of community, cultural, and societal improvement.

Everything is important. One of the biggest differences between what Unique Process Advisors like Scott do and what product-based advisors do lies in the ability to ask clients about everything in their lives. Unique Process Advisors are better able to ask these questions because they are paid directly up front by the clients to have these conversations. The advisor-client relationship is marked by creative problem-solving teamwork from the very start. Within this teamwork, everything that is important to the client is also important to the advisor.

- **Debra Schatzki:** *Financial Services In A Box*™
Debra, who lives and works New York City, loves the creative teamwork that her Unique Process produces. In her process, *Financial Services In A Box*, this transformed teamwork involves financial advisors working with accountants. Traditionally, these two kinds of advisors have often been wary of one another, but Debra has designed a comprehensive, integrative approach that enables accountants and advisors to jointly produce extraordinary results for their shared clientele.

Predictable development and expansion. Probably the greatest breakthrough that having a Unique Process provides lies in the predictability of building a growing, profitable business. All these Unique Process Advisors are thinking in terms of ten-

and twenty-year futures of development and expansion. This is in stark contrast with most product-based advisors, who worry about the next quarter's results. Unique Process Advisors have businesses with predictable cash flow and profits, and ever-increasing opportunities for new sources of revenue.

• Tom Miller: *The VisionLink Solution*™

Tom Miller, from Laguna Beach, California, has seen his overall business grow steadily since he organized it around his *VisionLink Solution*. Tom's clients are privately-owned businesses with revenues between $20 million and $200 million. The VisionLink process enables business owners to use compensation of employees as one of their most effective growth strategies. Within his Unique Process, Tom and his network of consultants become crucial growth advisors to thousands of businesses that create large numbers of new jobs in the U.S. every year.

Talented people are attracted. Tom told us that one of the great advantages of having a formalized Unique Process lies in the ability to attract and keep great staff members. Other Unique Process Advisors have made the same point. This advantage cannot be overestimated in a labor market where the competition for skilled employees is becoming more intense every year. The Unique Process, in addition to making "Front Stage" relationships with clientele more creative and rewarding, also helps enormously in making the "Back Stage" relationships with staff members more productive and lasting. Every stage of a Unique Process provides a focused area of skill development and an opportunity for the growth of responsibility, authority, and compensation. It provides employees within a Unique Process business with a blueprint for long-term success and satisfaction.

• Charlie Epstein: *The 401k Coach® Program*

Charlie Epstein, from Springfield, Massachusetts, has seen how his *401k Coach Program* has enabled him to build a powerful team. He is clear that this would never have been possible if his business was still based entirely on selling commoditized products. Charlie's "team" not only includes those who work within his personal business, but hundreds of other financial advisors who use The 401k Coach platform to grow their own businesses. At a time when the issue of retirement income for tens of millions of American workers is a growing issue, Charlie Epstein has designed a solution that can bring "paychecks for life" to millions of individuals who are worried about their security.

Other advisors sign on. Charlie Epstein's 401k Coach network illustrates something that often happens with Unique Process Advisors: *Other advisors want to license the packaged wisdom and creativity of the Unique Process to grow their own businesses.* Dan Taylor, Mary Anne Ehlert, Lee Brower, Scott Keffer, Debra Schatzki, and Tom Miller are providing the same kind of opportunity in their areas that Charlie is providing for his advisors in the retirement income field. In this way, Unique Process Advisors are replacing large bureaucratic organizations as the main teachers and providers of cutting-edge concepts, methods, and tools for financial advisors in the 21st-century marketplace.

• Doug Andrew: *The True Wealth Transformer*™

Doug, from Salt Lake City, has developed a Unique Process that is transforming the business capabilities of thousands of financial advisors, lawyers, accountants, real estate agents, and mortgage brokers. His *True Wealth Transformer* process is now arguably the single biggest source of new life insurance premiums in the United States. The insight that gave rise to

Doug's process was that most Americans' wealth is passively locked in their personal homes. Over a period of decades, they miss the opportunity to create millions more in personal assets. According to Doug, the normal approach to home ownership means that millions of people end up "missing a fortune." *The True Wealth Transformer* enables individuals to utilize the value of their home assets to also purchase life insurance with tax-protected and creditor-proof returns.

Giant agents of creative change. Doug Andrew, like all the advisors here, created his Unique Process to transform his own business. The increases in productivity and profitability were immediate and dramatic. In achieving these breakthroughs, Doug realized that he had created a means for other financial advisors to do the same for their businesses. As a result, he created a training and licensing program that has now attracted thousands of participants. As his network of advisors expanded, all using his Unique Process, large insurance companies came knocking. The executives and managers of these corporations recognized that the *True Wealth Transformer* process had introduced an entirely new way to market life insurance in large volumes. Doug's creativity has now brought about a third transformation. By enabling a large number of insurance agents to sell in a new way, he has changed both the way these companies think about their marketplace and the way they design their insurance products. *This exemplifies a general lesson about the 21st-century financial services marketplace: Individuals with innovative ideas can become giant agents of creative change.*

• Rob Darnbrough: *The Second Chance Program*™
Rob, who lives and works in Vancouver, B.C., is another financial advisor who saw a great advantage and opportunity in helping other financial advisors. Because of a severe constriction of

re-insurance underwriting in Canada, many large case agents across the country were having difficulty securing coverage for their clients. The large Canadian insurance companies were not providing any immediate solutions to this issue, so Rob developed his own approach to solve the problem for his own personal clientele. Using his advantage as a dual citizen of Canada and the U.S., he approached American companies with a major new source of high-quality insurance business: cases that had been declined north of the border. The U.S. companies found this appealing and accepted the cases he couldn't get placed in Canada. Once he solved the problem for his own business, he turned to helping other agents. The resulting Unique Processs, *The Second Chance Program*, has now become the single biggest underwriting alternative for dozens of top Canadian insurance agents.

Better for everyone. Rob's innovative solution for other agents underscores a trend among Unique Process Advisors: They use their creativity to make things better for everyone. This goes against the grain of self-centered competitiveness that is encouraged by the typical sales policies and practices in a commoditized financial industry. Because Rob has created a "Value Creation Monopoly" within his own business, and then with his *Second Chance Program*, he knows that it makes far more sense for other financial advisors to cooperate with him rather than compete against him.

• Betty Norman: *Life Perspective*™ *Financial Planning*
Betty, from Los Angeles, brings a lifetime of coaching and counseling experience and wisdom to her financial clientele. Since financial services was a second career for her, Betty decided that she wanted to do it differently. Instead of focusing on product sales, she concentrated her creativity on developing the "best lifetime perspectives" for her clients.

Out of these unique long-range perspectives, the appropriate mix of products and services emerged without Betty having to sell them. Her clientele loved it so much that she began charging separately for her Unique Process, which only increased the product sales. Confident that this approach worked for her, Betty, like the other advisors described here, has now packaged her Unique Process so it can be utilized by hundreds of other advisors who want to take the same "life perspectives" approach to their clientele.

Thousands of "positive monopolies." What our experience with Betty Norman and the other Unique Process Advisors has revealed is that there is unlimited room in the financial services marketplace for innovative client-focused financial advisors. Because of the way Unique Processes develop and expand, they very quickly provide their creators with "positive monopolies" that increasingly provide higher levels of productivity, as well as immunity to competition. This experience of achieving monopolies is one of the biggest surprises that Unique Process Advisors notice as they transform their business practices. Having been trained in an entirely commodity-based industry for many years, it often takes them a while to understand the strength and sustainability of what they've created. Let's examine this idea, which we call "Value Creation Monopoly," in the next section. Once financial advisors realize that they can achieve this extraordinary advantage, it becomes a central motivation.

IDEA 1

The Value Creation Monopoly

"That gave me a sense of power and opportunity I had never felt before. This realization also indicated how I could build an entirely different kind of financial practice. The new approach would give me much greater freedom and enjoyment."

The Value Creation Monopoly

Becoming crucial to people's future success.

A powerful insight occurred to Dan Taylor a number of years ago after he had had several unusually productive and satisfying meetings with clients.

"I realized that the things I knew about these people, what their issues were, and where they wanted to go with their lives, was something that none of the people in head offices knew about. That gave me a sense of power and opportunity I had never felt before. This realization also indicated how I could build an entirely different kind of financial practice. The new approach would give me much greater freedom and enjoyment."

The four advantages of having a Value Creation Monopoly.
Dan Taylor's brainstorm had to do with the unique advantages that thousands of other financial advisors are discovering they have in today's financial marketplace.

Within their relationships with many of their best clients and customers lies a potential "Value Creation Monopoly." This Value Creation Monopoly, once realized, can become the basis for an entirely different way of doing business.

Entrepreneurial: The biggest difference the monopoly makes is that it enables financial advisors to operate as pure entrepreneurs in a 21st-century financial services industry that is becoming more bureaucratic every day.

STRATEGIC FORMULA

VALUE CREATION MONOPOLY

8. TRANSFORMATIVE IMPACT

1. POWERFUL RELATIONSHIPS

2. UNIQUE WISDOM

3. UNIQUE PROCESS

4. INDEPENDENT INCOME

5. BYPASS REGULATIONS

6. CLIENT-FOCUSED

7. ENTREPRENEURIAL FREEDOM

Independent revenue: The realization of a Value Creation Monopoly enables financial advisors to create a growing revenue stream that is completely independent of regulated commissions, and even industry licenses.

Immunity from commoditization: The Value Creation Monopoly enables advisors to escape from commoditization. When they do sell products, they are able to do so free of competition from other advisors.

Predictable Unique Process: The monopoly enables financial advisors to transform all their business activities into one or more "Unique Processes" that provide a predictable, always improving, always more profitable approach to their professional careers.

When advisor Doug Andrew became aware that he could have these four strategic advantages in his financial business, he felt "incredibly liberated." He had spent 20 years as a life insurance agent dealing with "all the frustrations that come from selling a commodity in a bureaucratized industry."

"When I realized that I could develop my own entrepreneurial platform based on my unique understanding of client issues, that I could dramatically increase my income and satisfaction within this new kind of business, and that I could do all this without having an insurance license, it was the most free I had felt in my professional career."

The unique creative power and potential of client relationships. What Dan Taylor, Doug Andrew, and the other advisors featured in this book recognized was that the key to the personal and professional freedom they had always dreamed about had always been in their grasp. The key lay in the unique creative power of their best client relationships. These relationships had already given them a "monopoly" in the marketplace that they hadn't recognized or appreciated. The Value Creation Monopoly has its roots in three sources:

1. The advisor's commitment and creativity: In each case, the monopoly is established within their lengthy relationships with clients, during which they have demonstrated commitment and creativity, helping the clients to eliminate their dangers, take advantage of their opportunities, and maximize their own strengths.

2. In-depth conversations about clients' life issues: The Value Creation Monopoly arises out of the quality of in-depth conversations the advisors have enabled clients to have about all aspects of their lives.

3. The advisor becoming the most important "life coach": The monopoly is a product of the life planning that these skillful advisors do with their clients, out of which the clients see the advisor as their most important "life coach."

Mary Anne Ehlert came from a management position in banking before she became a financial advisor. What she came to understand was that, as an advisor, she had access to crucial knowledge about people's lives that made her uniquely able to help them with their most important issues.

"Having been in management, I know that people in these positions in financial services companies are usually unknowledgeable about what is occurring in the lives of clientele. Nothing that corporate managers do engenders a relationship with clients. None of it involves a conversation that reveals what clients are dealing with and trying to achieve in their lives. I realized, once I became an individual advisor, that I had an extraordinary creative advantage. I could develop solutions that were better than anything a large corporation could think of doing–an entirely different kind of value creation relationship."

Dan, Doug, and Mary Anne have all tapped into something powerful, creative, liberating, and—as we will see from their experiences and those of seven other financial advisors—something that has the potential to transform not only the financial services industry but important areas of society itself.

Advisor freedom comes from following a strategic formula.
In analyzing what the ten advisors featured in this book did, and also what hundreds of other advisors in Strategic Coach® are doing, we have identified a strategic formula (please refer to the diagram on page 23) that they all followed to transform their businesses:

They recognized that the uniquely powerful relationships they have with clientele are an unlimited source of creative freedom. This freedom comes from the fact that they have acquired extraordinary "transformative wisdom" from thousands of hours of unique conversations with their clients. This unique transformative wisdom is the foundation for creating a Unique Process. This Unique Process, as it develops, frees them from dependency on commoditized and regulated products. This freedom from products also means freedom from bureaucratic regulation and control. Everything in their business becomes about uniquely solving the crucial life issues of their clients. This enables advisors to move from bureaucratic dependency to entrepreneurial freedom. The more this entrepreneurial freedom grows, the greater their creative impact on the lives of others.

To get a clearer understanding how this formula takes root and develops in the practice of a single advisor, let's take a look at how Dan Taylor created his Parent Care Solution. Dan's creativity and success point out a common theme among Unique Process Advisors: The inspiration for creating their process often comes from a personal negative experience in life that disturbed or angered them. They then channeled their negative emotions into a creative solution that benefits many other people.

Dan Taylor
The Parent Care Solution™

All of our Unique Process Advisors had to make a key career decision: They could continue to sell other people's commodities, or they could become autonomous entrepreneurs with a private brand. Dan Taylor has had great success freeing himself from being a commoditized financial advisor, making him a role model for hundreds of other financial advisors attempting to do the same thing. Dan has trained and practiced as a lawyer, life insurance agent, and investment advisor over a 20-year career in Charlotte, North Carolina. He joined Strategic Coach as a client in 1993, and has since become a highly focused entrepreneur and the creator of a Unique Process called The Parent Care Solution™, which is a process that creates a platform for the long-term care of aging parents without financially or emotionally destroying the family. Dan is also the creator of The Divorce Mediation Program™.

Dan Sullivan: Let's begin by talking about how you got started with the whole idea of The Parent Care Solution. What was the experience that triggered your thinking?

Dan Taylor: Well, the experience that created The Parent Care Solution actually happened during the third year of taking care of my father. My father was stricken with Alzheimer's rather abruptly in the spring of 2000, and so I began a process of taking care of him in his care center from 2000 to 2005. In January of 2003, I woke up one morning and I thought, "I've got money, I've got a great support system, and here I am, on my knees, struggling with how to help my father." It occurred to me that if I was struggling, with all the advantages I have, what would rest of the world do in terms of facing this? So I just reverse-engineered it. I thought, "If I could do this over, what is the process I would like to go through? What's the experience,

what are the resources I would need, what's the process I would want to go through?" That's how I got creative.

> I was absolutely overwhelmed by the amount of partitioning and fragmentation that existed in the resources available to help me ... I didn't even really know how to begin the conversation with any-one about what I needed because I wasn't sure what I needed, and I didn't have the language.

Dan Sullivan: Dan, when you were putting the process together, what vision did you have in mind about the kind of communication that can go on between adults and their par-ents, who are now perhaps in their seventies or eighties?

Dan Taylor: Well, the ideal com-munication would have been one of increasing connection and collaboration and intimacy with my father around these transitional issues that he was going through. And I didn't see a mechanism out there from a conversation standpoint that enabled me to do that in a very integrated manner. The financial services industry tends to approach this subject from a product standpoint: Either it's long-term care, or it's health insurance, or it's survivor income life insurance. The legal industry tends to want a document solution, pieces of paper that enable certain things to happen. And, of course, the accounting industry tends to look at it simply from the tax-planning standpoint.

For its part, the medical industry tends to look at it in a purely reactive mode in the extreme. Or if they do any preemptive planning, it's what I call "the-last-train-out planning," meaning that there really isn't any discussion about the future. Instead, the person is told, "It's time for you to go to this train station, and your last train out is in about five years. So you just sort of hang out here until it comes." I wanted a conversation.

Then, when my father had to come and live with me for a short period of time, I was absolutely overwhelmed by the amount of partitioning and fragmentation that existed in the resources available to help me. In other words, I didn't even really know how to begin the conversation with anyone about what I needed because I wasn't sure what I needed, and I didn't have the language. On the day after my father came to live with me, I started calling care centers, retirement homes, nursing homes—because I thought they were all the same. So I had to learn the language. I also had to create a central resource platform that provided the tools for me to think about my father's care, as well as the resources I could access.

Dan Sullivan: You've had a lot of conversations with other people who have gone through The Parent Care Solution. What does going through the process actually do to their lives?
Dan Taylor: I think what it does is let them grasp the enormity of this potential problem from a "big picture" standpoint. Very often, people don't even know what the problem is. And this situation is so huge and it's so draconian that they don't even know how to begin thinking about it. So the conversations actually put the problem in a context that creates a possibility of solving at least 80 percent of the problems.

Dan Sullivan: Dan, talk to me about the conversations. I know that you've broken your process down into a series of different conversations.
Dan Taylor: The conversations are really fixed, Dan, and they start from a broad-based, non-threatening view of the future, to a much more intimate conversation about how people want to be perceived. One of the mistakes made in talking to parents about aging is that people begin the conversations in a very intrusive, abrupt way. For example, I read an article two years ago about how to talk to your parents about retirement, and the author suggested that you bring it up over dinner. I started laughing hysterically because I could imagine sitting

with my father in 1996 at Christmas dinner saying, "Would you like some turkey, would you like some more broccoli, and, by the way, have you thought about the nursing home?" And that's the way we are taught to do it.

What I did was to divide the issues that parents and their children face into seven different conversations that we call The C.A.R.E. Conversations™. These conversations cover about 80 percent of what the children are going to have to deal with in relation to their parents' care. The first conversation is called The Big Picture Conversation™, and it focuses on the challenges that the parents see as they contemplate their future. It also looks at the alternatives or options they see for managing those challenges, the resources they can access to meet those challenges, and the experience they would like to create for themselves and others if they could successfully overcome those challenges. This structure is followed throughout the rest of the conversations.

The second conversation is The Money Conversation™. The goal here is to discover how much money they have, where it is, what it's doing, and how it can be used to finance their future as they age. The third conversation is called The Facility Conversation™. It is a conversation to determine where the parents see themselves living as they transition through the various stages of aging and care. For example, we know that the vast majority of people want to stay in their homes as long as they can, but they have to use some foresight and planning in order to do that. In The Facility Conversation, we are trying to get them to see all the options available to them, including their own home, a retirement community, assisted living, special care, and so on.

The next conversation is what we call The Attention Conversation™. It's been my experience, with my father and in watching people at the nursing home interact with their children, that people in a care facility are desperately lonely. Their friends are aging, and some of them have died. Many times, they are in a facility that's far away from their community, and they never had a conversation with their children about the kind of attention they wanted from their family as they aged. In my situation, I went to my father's care center every Saturday and Sunday for five years and helped serve breakfast. It was a way for me to not only interact with him, but to interact with other people who didn't have visitors. You know, huge numbers of people living in these centers have no visitors at all. So The Attention Conversation is about relationship.

A really important conversation is The House Conversation™. For most people, their home represents safety, security, memories, and hope for the future. It is critical that you ascertain how they feel about their home and what their intentions are concerning it. The house as a financial asset represents a significant percentage of an aging parent's financial picture. Changing regulations for Medicaid and other government assistance may dictate that house decisions are made in a different light and much sooner than ever before. This is one of the most important conversations that parents can have, not only for themselves but for the children's inheritance possibilities.

The Property Conversation™ is about who they want to leave their things to, and why it's important they make those decisions. In many ways, we define ourselves in the U.S. by our possessions. So the watch, the ring, the rocking chair—all of these things are part of that. We want to pass them on to other people as a way of remembering us.

The final conversation is The Legacy Conversation™, which is really about how we want to be remembered—how we want to be thought of, what we have contributed that is important to us, and what we want to perpetuate about those contributions going forward. And so, when you look at the conversations, they really go from a broad big-picture view down to something really intimate, like how others will remember you.

Dan Sullivan: Dan, I couldn't help but think as you were going through the seven conversations that, in fact, this is a three-generation educational program.

Dan Taylor: I believe that our Parent Care Specialists and financial advisors who choose to work in this area will practice on a generation that was the subject of Tom Brokaw's book, *The Greatest Generation*. In addition, they will implement these ideas with the boomers and their children because boomers are more open to these types of conversations than perhaps their parents are.

Dan Sullivan: Let's say a fifty-year-old couple has this conversation with their parents on both sides, who are in their seventies or eighties. That's two generations, but the fifty-year-olds, having gone through this conversation with their parents, are now also totally prepared to go through this conversation with their children.

Dan Taylor: I had this conversation with my step-daughter, Ashley, over the holidays. I talked with her about the fact that she has a father, and part of her responsibility is to pay attention to him as he ages. But one of her issues is that she has spent a big part of her life with me. So I wanted to talk to her about my expectations in that area and my goals, and, you know, it wasn't as structured because she is nineteen years old. But what we were able to talk about was, "Look, here is how I would like to be in a relationship with you, and here is what I have done to prepare financially and emotionally for that time so that a large part of that responsibility is not on you." I absolutely think it's a tool for the boomer generation.

Dan Sullivan: So consequently, if there is widespread use of The Parent Care Solution in society, you are actually solving the problem at its toughest level, which is with the oldest generation, who were given to understand that the government and the corporations were going to take care of them. Then the middle generation, who are in their fifties, were given to understand that the government and corporations were going to take care of them. And my belief is that the generation that's in their twenties and thirties now know that nobody is going to take care of them.

... the decline of the defined benefit retirement plan business in the U.S. is a real signal that corporate America wants to shift the responsibility for our future retirement income and make it our responsibility instead of theirs.

Dan Taylor: In fact, our government is really putting the signs up. If you think of this as a highway, we have already passed signs that say "Road Out," "Shoulder Gone," "Cliff Ahead" — and more road signs are appearing every day. It's very clear to me that the boomer generation will more or less be indexed out of traditional social security, that it will become an entitlement system for the lower economic portions of society.

New savings accounts that have been introduced are simply a way for the government and corporations to shift more and more of the healthcare responsibility to individuals. You know, the decline of the defined benefit retirement plan business in the U.S. is a real signal that corporate America wants to shift the responsibility for our future retirement income and make it our responsibility instead of theirs.

Dan Sullivan: Dan, tell me how other advisors get involved with The Parent Care Solution, because it's such a huge program with infinite possibilities.

Dan Taylor: We've created a training course to teach people how to use these conversations and a complete capability for them to implement this inside their practice. Right now, we have about 30 licensed Parent Care Specialists around the country. For the training, they come to Charlotte, North Carolina, and spend a couple of days in what we call The Parent Care University™. We teach them all the structural issues about aging that give them the conversation technology and the implementation capabilities to take back and use with their existing and potential clients.

Dan Sullivan: You've had a chance to look at the type of advisors who are showing up for this. Is there a pattern emerging?
Dan Taylor: I'm seeing the seasoned practitioners, people who have been in the business for longer than five years but have an older clientele. They are pretty evenly coming from the life insurance industry, the asset management business, the accounting industry, and the legal industry. Our last workshop had two accountants, an attorney, one person who only practices in life insurance, and two financial planners with emphasis in asset management.

Dan Sullivan: From the experiences of the advisors who have been out there so far, what difference has it made to their practices? These are probably veteran people who started by learning how to sell products and then moved more and more toward relationship-based careers. What has the inclusion of The Parent Care Solution done to their practices?
Dan Taylor: On our website, *www.parentcaresolution.com*, we have comments from the advisors who have gone through the program. I think the comments speak for the program itself, and all of these advisors are open to being contacted by anyone who wants to go through the program. These advisors are beginning to implement The Parent Care Solution inside their practices, starting with their existing clients, and what they are seeing is the huge platform opportunity this concept offers in connecting their older clients and their children with the advisor and his or her practice.

One of the dangers we're trying to eliminate for financial advisors is a result of most of the industry's seasoned practitioners being over the age of forty. If they're not careful, they'll be spending most of their time developing client relationships that the children's advisors will then take over because the advisors of the parents don't have relationships with the children.

Dan Sullivan: Certainly The Parent Care Solution would automatically create a client base where you get three generations out of one process.

Dan Taylor: I believe it's possible to use the strategy of The Parent Care Solution to make multi-generational wealth preservation and transfer planning a reality. Traditionally, practitioners have hoped that if they did a good job for the parents, somehow the children would recognize that and use them as their advisor as well. In order to do that, there has to be a connecting structure and strategy beyond the traditional asset management services. There is a strong possibility that the asset management business will be completely commoditized within the next five years. Those advisors who want to retain the children as clients will have to offer more than those types of services. I believe The Parent Care Solution is a connecting strategy for the advisor to maintain the relationship with the older clients, initiate a relationship with the children of those clients (the boomers), and set the stage for continued conversations with the boomers' children.

Dan Sullivan: So when you think about it, it really does take into account a two- or three-decade time frame.

Dan Taylor: There is a combination of things coming together that I think creates the perfect storm for this: Simply, for the first time in history, we have three generations existing in the same time frame, and that's an unusual phenomenon prior to the information age. So you have the seniors, you have the boomers, you have the boomers' children, and in many cases you have the great-grandchildren of the seniors all alive at the same time.

I believe the presence of three and, in some cases, four generations living at the same time is contributing to the focus on this subject. I also believe that technology, the microchip, is enabling us to manage all the financial, legal, and medical affairs of an individual from one common data aggregation platform. Whether it's a platform like eMoney Advisor, Fidelity's Retirement Income Planner, or the other data aggregation software that is emerging, we are on the verge of being able to globally oversee all of a client's needs. But in their best evolution, all of these platforms are simply technology. What is really needed is a Unique Process, like The Parent Care Solution, that provides the leadership, relationship, and creativity that people need.

The Solutions Center on our website is a one-stop shop with access to parent care resources. It offers asset management, trust services, care companions, and a parent care channel. It actually is a total resource for boomers and parents.

Dan Sullivan: Dan, we're looking at a problem that has only been nipped at the edges by most people. Hardly anyone has gone right to the center of this issue. I think that's the power of what you've done. It's very clear to me that the passion you have for this really comes out of your personal experience and the pain that you went through. You've created a process from that pain to help an enormous number of other people going through that same pain themselves.

Dan Taylor: I think that financial advisors are really well equipped because they have very intimate, connected conversations with people. But I also see the opportunity for advisors to collaborate and partner with the legal and accounting industries around this concept to create a whole new support mechanism for boomers, their parents, and their children that has never existed before. This particular process really offers the opportunity, more than any process that's out there, for teams of advisors to collaborate for the mutual benefit of their client.

Dan Sullivan: Dan, what's this done for you personally? Going back to 2003 when you were really deep into the problem area, caring for your own father, what has the creation of The Parent Care Solution done for you?

Dan Taylor: Well, first, the creation of it during that time period up until my father passed in 2005 gave me hope. I actually created the program to work myself out of a hole that I had gotten into emotionally over the enormous stress and pressure of this. I wanted more than anything to transform my own experience by creating something that other people, and I, could use. Second, as I travel around the country—and I'll speak about The Parent Care Solution 30 times this year—the lights are coming on in advisors' eyes about the big picture and the big possibilities they have ahead of them. So as a practitioner in the industry and a resident of the industry for almost 25 years, I am beginning to see people getting excited. They see a future out there in areas like The Parent Care Solution and the other Unique Processes that Unique Process Advisors are offering to help them succeed in business.

... I also see the opportunity for advisors to collaborate and partner with the legal and the accounting industry around this concept to create a whole new support mechanism for boomers and their parents and their children that has never existed before. This particular process really offers the opportunity, more than any process that's out there, for teams of advisors to collaborate for the mutual benefit of their client.

For contact details on The Parent Care Solution, please see page 233.

IDEA 2

Packaging And Selling Personal Wisdom

"The moment I started charging, everything changed in the quality of the relationships, from start to finish. The clients wanted to reach a solution as quickly as possible because they were already financially and emotionally committed. Of course, I had to demonstrate right at the beginning the value I was going to create, and that forced me to package my process."

Packaging And Selling Personal Wisdom

Charging for what people value most.

Dan Taylor describes his excitement when he realized that he could get paid for his own ideas:

"I was trained like everyone to believe that my only value as a financial advisor was in terms of the products that the companies provided to me. Then one day I decided to charge an extra fee up front for all the wisdom and creativity that I was going to put into a very complex case. The prospect asked me to write up a proposal outlining what I was going to do and what results were going to be produced. In 24 hours, I was back with my first Unique Process. The man wrote me the check and later wrote much bigger checks for the insurance and investments that were involved in my eventual solution. I was amazed at the difference that getting paid extra and up-front made to my confidence. It was like being in a completely different business. After that, I always presented my work as a Unique Process that required an upfront fee in addition to the commissions I would make from the eventual product sales."

Dan Taylor's experience with getting paid extra for a Unique Process is similar to hundreds of other financial advisors who are also reporting breakthroughs in their businesses. There are two important points to emphasize in all of these experiences.

One, charging clients an upfront fee immediately makes them into committed creative partners in a working relationship. Two, clients will only pay up front if they can see a formalized

REQUIREMENT	PAY-OFF
A formalized and custom-designed problem-solving process that transforms clients' special issues.	Clients become active and committed partners in an exclusive, creative relationship.

Make yourself different in every way.

Make it about questions, discoveries, and breakthroughs.

Make it about all of their transformations.

Make it about their dangers, opportunities, and strengths.

Make it an evolving process that keeps getting better.

Make it visual and memorable.

problem-solving process that relates to their specific issues. Let's examine each of these points in terms of how they transform the entire way of doing business for financial advisors.

Clients become active, committed partners in a relationship.
Scott Keffer told us how surprised he was at the quality of his client relationships after he had received his first upfront check for his initial Unique Process:

"It was just totally different. Like a lot of agents, I was always told that I had to earn the client's business by putting in a lot of time and effort for free. I now realize what a demeaning experience this is, that prospects actually lose respect for you when you do valuable work for them up front but don't charge. The moment I started charging, everything changed in the quality of the relationships, from start to finish. The clients wanted to reach a solution as quickly as possible because they were already financially and emotionally committed. Of course, I had to demonstrate the value I was going to create right at the beginning, and that forced me to package my process."

A formalized problem-solving process that relates to client issues.
If getting paid an extra fee dramatically changes the way that financial advisors see their business, so does having a formalized Unique Process. By formalized, I mean that it is "packaged." Debra Schatzki describes the turning point that occurred the moment she understood what it meant to package her wisdom and creativity:

"My real excitement as an advisor came from having all of my clients being more excited about their opportunities and futures. And after I helped them to do that once, I wanted to keep doing it for the long run. I couldn't form a long-term relationship based on products. It had to be something else. Then it hit me, after one of my clients told me that the reason he worked with me was because he did his best thinking when I

was asking him questions. He said he was more confident about his future when he was around me. So it occurred to me, why not get paid for my questions? Why not get paid for my unique approach to solving complex situations? Why not get paid for my ability to get people excited about their futures? After that, instead of selling insurance and investments, I started selling myself in the form of my own uniquely packaged process of thinking. What amazed me was that when I started doing this, the product sales became much, much larger."

Packaging your thinking and getting paid for it.
Over the years since these initial experiences, Dan, Scott, and Debra have all become masters of "packaging their thinking" and getting paid for it. Their successful experiences, and those of hundreds of other financial advisors in Strategic Coach, have created a growing knowledge base about how to do this. It's something that any experienced and skillful financial advisor can do, and do quickly, but it works best by observing the following guidelines:

• **Make yourself different in every way possible:** Set yourself completely apart from other advisors who sell commoditized products that all sound and work the same, as they represent large, impersonal organizations that all look and act the same.

• **Make it about questions, discoveries, and breakthroughs:** Industry-trained advisors are taught to have an answer for every question. Differentiate yourself by asking great questions that enable prospects and clients to think, see, and respond to things in totally new ways.

• **Make it about investment and partnership:** The financial services industry teaches advisors to invest enormous time and effort for free with the possibility of getting paid at the end for a product sale. Differentiate yourself by asking the prospect or client to invest up front in your unique thinking process. This payment turns your relationship into an active, creative partnership.

- **Make it about their transformations:** Most financial advisors only sell technical solutions. Differentiate yourself by creating transformative solutions—that is, breakthroughs that make clients feel a greater sense of direction, confidence, and capability in all areas of their lives.

- **Make it about their dangers, opportunities, and strengths:** Most financial advisors go into their first meeting talking about themselves, their experience, and their successes. Differentiate yourself by only talking about the client, and only about three things: the dangers that worry them, the opportunities that excite them, and their existing strengths that give them confidence.

- **Make it about an evolving process that keeps getting better:** Product-based advisors can only think about selling a product so they can get paid. Differentiate yourself by "selling" great thinking and effective actions within a formal process that keeps getting better over the years.

- **Make it visual and memorable:** The vast majority of advisors deal only in words, either spoken or written. Differentiate yourself by presenting all of your ideas and solutions in the form of powerful and memorable graphics.

Mary Anne Ehlert is a textbook example of how to differentiate yourself, using your packaged wisdom and creativity. Let's look at how she has done this.

Mary Anne Ehlert
The Process For Protected Tomorrows™

An Industry Transformer™ in the financial services industry is an entrepreneurial advisor who innovates new forms of value creation that not only transform his or her own business, but offer the possibility for many other advisors to transform theirs. In the last interview, we featured Dan Taylor, creator of The Parent Care Solution. In this interview, I am pleased to introduce Mary Anne Ehlert, a highly successful and universally respected financial advisor. Mary Anne has created an extraordinarily useful Unique Process called The Process For Protected Tomorrows™, which provides lifetime support for families who care for special-needs individuals.

Dan Sullivan: I'm really excited about this interview, Mary Anne, because your story is an inspiring example of how financial advisors can be a positive force for social change. Now I want to discuss the origins of Protected Tomorrows. Could you talk a little about what brought you to this idea?

Mary Anne Ehlert: Well, I started out in banking and was there for 20 years, but after one of my jobs was to lay off 1,500 people in two days, I decided at that point that I really wanted to start making a difference in people's lives. At first I thought it would be retirement planning. But when I started up a business and opened my doors, I found that I was doing the same thing as everyone else.

Dan Sullivan: You joined the Strategic Coach Program.

Mary Anne Ehlert: Yes. And when we began to talk about Unique Ability®, I found that all the other financial advisors were really stuck on thinking their Unique Ability® had to do with the products they offered. They thought their Unique Ability® was around insurance, or annuities, and so on. Instead of focusing on the products, I focused on the needs of my clients, and I realized that my first clients were really my parents. They were

having some anxiety about Marcia, my sister with a disability. They were scared that they were going to die and leave my sister alone. So we talked it through, and it became very clear to me that as an advisor, I needed to devote myself to coming up with solutions for people with disabilities.

Dan Sullivan: Could you stop for a second, Mary Anne, and talk a little about Marcia and your experience growing up in a special-needs family?

Mary Anne Ehlert: Sure. I grew up in a large family with two older brothers and three younger sisters. And one of those sisters was Marcia, who had cerebral palsy. Marcia had to be dressed and had to be helped with food, so she really consumed a lot of our energy. We didn't do the things that most normal kids do. We didn't take vacations, we didn't go to restaurants. Marcia really became the guiding force in our family life. Every holiday revolved around her, and this is still the case today even though she's gone.

Dan Sullivan: How close were you to Marcia?

Mary Anne Ehlert: It's interesting because Marcia had a twin, but everyone always said that I was her twin in spirit. We were really close emotionally. It was me who convinced my parents to let her go and live residentially. She lived in a residential environment the last few years of her life and died at the age of 39. But as I said, she's still a major center of attention in the family.

Dan Sullivan: How has this experience impacted you on a broad level?

Mary Anne Ehlert: It has totally changed the way I think. I have a nice home, and I have nice stuff, but what really matters is family. Marcia taught me this. It really has impacted the kinds of friends I have because, going back to childhood, if someone didn't accept my sister, they weren't going to be my friend. So in my business, it's Marcia who inspires me to do more than just sell products and make money. And I've learned we can really make change in the world, in a way no one else believed could be done.

Dan Sullivan: Now with your own experience in mind, what are the main dangers for people who have relatives with special needs—the dangers that your process is designed to address?
Mary Anne Ehlert: Number one, there's the fear that you're not going to be there for that person, whether it is your child, your parent, or your spouse. Most fears revolve around care: Who is going to take care of the individual with special needs, where will he live, who is going to feed and clothe him? From a legal perspective, there are all the legal documents that need to be put in place, and this is often very overwhelming for the family. There are a lot of opportunities for funding and grants, but there's the danger that the paperwork will fall through the cracks. Also, there is a real danger that the guardian will do all the planning but die without leaving clear instructions. Finally, there are emotional dangers: Some family members are in denial about the disability, and some have problems communicating their feelings.

Dan Sullivan: Clients will walk into your office with all of these dangers. Why don't you outline the Unique Process you've devised to serve them?
Mary Anne Ehlert: Well, first I want to clarify that the process is especially designed for parents who have children with disabilities, but it can also be used for spouses or other family members with disabilities.

The first step of the process we call Take A Candid Look™. This is in the first meeting, where we ask the client to be honest with us and with themselves, and describe the disability, describe the financial situation, describe the reality of funding the child: Is it going to be like sending your child to Harvard for the rest of his or her life? How are you going to do that? These are the questions that the client has probably tried to

… once we've wrapped our arms around the parents and made sure they have a future to look forward to, we can develop a life plan for the person with special needs.

avoid, so once they start to openly discuss them, we can move on to the next stage.

In the second step, Create The Future Map™, we put in place a life plan for the parents and the other family members. Before we even talk about the child with the disability, we plan for the other children's college education and for the parents' retirement. Then we put the child with the disability into the picture and ask, "Okay, how do they fit into everything you need to do for yourself?" So once we've wrapped our arms around the parents and made sure they have a future to look forward to, we can develop a life plan for the person with special needs.

In the Filter The Legal Options™ step, we take the client to the appropriate attorney and help them handle their wills, their trusts, their special-needs trusts, and any guardianship or custody issues.

In Step 4, Capture Potential Benefits™, we determine if a child is eligible for SSI income or Medicare or Medicaid. Each state has different services and procedures, and we help the family navigate the confusing bureaucracy and find case workers.

We've created a book, *My Special Life®*, which is developed during the step Document The Wonder™. Here, the family can write the history of their child, and we are also now putting it online. This is the fifth step. The book talks about the child's medical history, religious history, what triggers the child, how the child socializes. This comforts the parents because they know that if they pass away, the new guardian will have all of this information. Future guardians will not feel alone and confused.

We call Step 6 Begin The Transition™. The transition to residential living is one of the most important events for a child with special needs. The schools are supposed to facilitate this, but they simply can't do it. So we run transition seminars where we bring similar sets of parents together. We're taking the life plan and actually building the child's future with residential, employment, and social life. There are all sorts of other programs that have come out of this; for example, we've formed recreation and employment support groups.

Fund The Future™ is the final step. This is where we coordinate a financial plan to achieve the vision that was laid out in Steps 1 to 6. This is where we figure out what insurance and investment products are most appropriate for the client. By that time, they have already given us all of their money. They have already said, "Here is my Merrill Lynch Account, and here is my Smith Barney account. And, here, take over my health insurance, my car insurance, my life insurance. You guys just handle everything."

Our process is supported by people, systems, technology. We have created one of the first online search tools to help families share critical information as a result of our process.

Dan Sullivan: You know, that's really interesting, Mary Anne, when you consider how most advisors are just taught to sell financial products. In your process, the products only become a significant topic in Step 7.
Mary Anne Ehlert: Yes. And our financial advisory advocates are selling more product than I ever used to before the process. But that piece is such a small piece that when we get to that step, we don't ever have to ask for it. It's handed to us. They're saying, "Please, you manage my money because you're the only one who understands my situation."

Dan Sullivan: Now, your process is very transformative, Mary

Anne, and I see you moving into several industries besides financial services: the education industry, the legal industry, and the medical industry. Could you elaborate?

Mary Anne Ehlert: Absolutely. First of all, I've already mentioned that schools are supposed to be running the transition programs, but they simply can't do it. We're walking in, and we're doing that. We have trained teachers, social workers, medical professionals, trainers, and, most recently, retired professionals who want to continue making a difference in the lives of many.

Dan Sullivan: What about the legal industry?

Mary Anne Ehlert: Well, we are obviously not attorneys, but we do work closely with a lot of attorneys. It's interesting because it often seems that we're more knowledgeable on certain subjects than they are. I've had several conversations with attorneys making $400 an hour where I am literally coordinating with them about what to write to make their document more flexible to meet the needs of these families. We now have attorneys calling us who have clients who don't want to work with them until they have talked to us first.

Dan Sullivan: The last one is the medical industry.

Mary Anne Ehlert: I had a man in my office the other day who had gone for 15 years denying that his son with autism had a disability and trying to prove that it was something physical instead of mental. He had never taken his son to the proper doctors or therapists for autism. At the beginning of the meeting, he was denying his son had a disability, and by the end, we had finally persuaded him to admit it. This was the first time that he had ever done that. We were also able to direct him to the proper medical professionals for autism. So though we're not doctors, we often play a role as medical consultants.

Dan Sullivan: You may not be a medical doctor, Mary Anne, but I certainly see you as a counselor, and not just a financial counselor.

Mary Anne Ehlert: I will tell you, Dan, that many of the parents who have been working with us have dropped their counseling. They say, "I get more out of my meeting with you than I do with counseling." Sometimes they even call us on the phone and talk about their anxieties. We aren't trained social workers, but we understand their situation.

Dan Sullivan: Well, a big part of my vision is that financial advisors in the 21st century will increasingly be the number one coaches for millions of people, and you're really a good example of how this can happen, Mary Anne.
Mary Anne Ehlert: Thank you.

Dan Sullivan: Now, I want to switch gears a little because not only do you have a revolutionary process, you have begun to spread that process to other advisors. Why don't you talk a little about how this all came about?
Mary Anne Ehlert: Over the years, I've done a lot of public speaking, and I've had many advisors come up to me and say, "I want to do what you're doing." There are a lot of advisors out there in their upper thirties, forties, and fifties who have made it on their own and made good money, but now they want to do something different. So I've designed a program to teach them my process.

Dan Sullivan: It's a licensing agreement, right?
Mary Anne Ehlert: Yes. Advisors pay a $5,000 licensing fee to be in the program. The first two years, there is an additional training fee. They learn how to use the process, and we give them the rights to use it, but they do not own it. The other thing we provide is a high-level research team to help advisors in various states figure out who the good attorneys are, what services are available, and what the procedures

> The numbers are just absolutely huge. There are over 54 million people with a disability in the U.S. alone.

are. For a fee, we will also help complete various applications for their clients.

Dan Sullivan: What is your criteria for participation in this program because I know you don't take just anybody?
Mary Anne Ehlert: Well, we are being very selective, and the advisors like it that way. We don't want people who are commission-based and come in all hungry to sell. We want successful advisors who are looking for a purpose, and they must either have a disabled family member or have worked in a facility for the disabled. I really believe in this requirement, and every person on my staff has also had some experience with a disabled individual.

Dan Sullivan: How many families are out there, Mary Anne? I mean families with a special-needs case, because the potential market for your process just seems limitless.
Mary Anne Ehlert: The numbers are just absolutely huge. There are over 54 million people with a disability in the U.S. alone.

Dan Sullivan: Following your model, there's just so much potential for bypassing what's happening in your industry because the demographics support everything you're doing. My question, then, is, how did your head office react to your process?
Mary Anne Ehlert: There were problems on the compliance end. I mean, I did a ton of volume, and it was fine when I was making them money, but when I started teaching other advisors, it was like I'd crossed a line. I was leaving their world, and they couldn't tolerate it. When I presented them with the teaching system, they said, "This is really great, but it will probably take us three years to get it approved." And I said, "I'm not waiting three years. I'm ready to go." I gave them the pitch at head office, and some people were really excited. But the constant refrain was, "It's great, but how can we control it?"

Dan Sullivan: That's not surprising.

Mary Anne Ehlert: They didn't want to lose me. I was their biggest producer on the securities side. They tried to leave me alone so I stayed, but that became increasingly difficult. I mean, I tried to restructure the contract with them, and the auditor came in. The auditor actually agreed with my idea, but after he filed his report, he got a call from compliance, and they said, "She can't do that." And my reaction was, "Yes I can, just not in your world." At that point, my business certainly didn't depend on them. And, of course, now I'm fully independent.

Dan Sullivan: Well, you'd just totally outgrown everything head office had to offer, Mary Anne. You don't talk product, and that's all they talk.

Mary Anne Ehlert: That's right. You can't focus on the individual when you are focusing on the product. My job is to figure out if a client needs insurance or investments and how much he needs, not what product pays the best commission. When people used to find out that we had the biggest book of business on the securities side, they would ask me about an insurance product and say, "What did you make on that?" I would say, "I don't know. My numbers people do that." They'd look at me like I was nuts. They'd ask me how I got so much business, and I'd say, "I don't talk product, I talk life story."

Dan Sullivan: Looking forward, Mary Anne, where do you see yourself taking Protected Tomorrows?

Mary Anne Ehlert: For a while, I was just doing the individual training program, but now I'm going to a different level and offering corporate licenses to major financial institutions. We are now talking to both financial institutions who need to train their select financial advisors and national disability groups who want to help their families. We believe we have something unique that will change the

> They ask me how I get so much business, and I say, "I don't talk product, I talk life story."

way families with special needs are serviced. We are just about ready to kick off Phase II. This will give access to our process to families online, driving thousands of families to those licensed with us. We now have solutions for all types of families so none of them has to feel alone or confused. We will be able to deliver service directly to the families, giving our advocates more time to see people.

Dan Sullivan: That's just phenomenal, Mary Anne.

Mary Anne Ehlert: You know, Dan, something that has been really important in all this has been to build up my team. They've really freed me up to work more on some of my passions—like finding a solution to the residential issue, because right now the government is just incapable of serving the disabled in this regard. I also helped to start a not-for-profit called the Special Needs Network that is a resource and support network for special-needs families. I'm starting to get in front of some influential people, so there are some really heartening developments on the activism side.

Dan Sullivan: You've been in the Strategic Coach Program for a while, Mary Anne, and also in Coach2*. How has this participation contributed to your development?

Mary Anne Ehlert: If I wasn't in the Coach, I would still be sitting in my home office seeing people one on one. It has helped me to figure out that I didn't need all my other businesses, that I just needed to focus on this process. The more I've focused on this market, the busier I've become. It helped me get through my sister's death. I had Coach the week after she died. You told me to write down what I learned from her, and this helped me figure out that she was my guiding path. I never thought I could do what I'm doing. I originally did not have family support on this one. I certainly didn't have head office support. What I have had, though, is the support of my team, and Strategic Coach is really responsible for teaching me the importance of investing in a team.

    *For the definition of Coach2, please see page 228.

Dan Sullivan: What about Coach2®?

Mary Anne Ehlert: It's the people and the ideas and the encouragement that make Coach2 special. The energy is just phenomenal. And Strategic Coach helps me keep thinking of new ways to deliver services. There are no limitations to our thinking and therefore no limits to our solutions.

> When the client comes in and says, "You are part of the family. We couldn't have survived without you" — well, it really doesn't get any better than that for a financial advisor.

Dan Sullivan: I want to compliment you, Mary Anne, because what you're doing is really remarkable. You're really the consummate Industry Transformer™ because your process has the potential to attract a lot of disgruntled advisors.

Mary Anne Ehlert: That's right. And it doesn't matter if it's an insurance person, an investment person, or even if the advisor has a license. If they care about these issues, and they are tired of the daily grind as a product salesperson, then my process would be very fulfilling for them.

Dan Sullivan: I want to conclude by asking you what Protected Tomorrows has done for your entire outlook as an advisor.

Mary Anne Ehlert: I've gotten so much payback from it. Sure, the financial payback has been great, but whenever a client comes in, I always remind myself that I also get psychological income. When the client comes in and says, "You are part of the family. We couldn't have survived without you"—well, it really doesn't get any better than that for a financial advisor.

For contact details on The Process For Protected Tomorrows, please see page 232.

IDEA 3

Choosing Clients Over Commissions

"And once you choose the client, it's amazing how liberated your thinking becomes. All of your client relationships blossom. But if you choose the products and commissions as your biggest priority, then, I believe, as an advisor, you become increasingly trapped, and your future starts to diminish."

Idea 3

Choosing Clients
Over Commissions

Differentiating yourself from everyone else.

Dan Taylor remembers a conversation that led to the biggest decision of his advisor career:

"I was at one of my Strategic Coach workshops in 1998, and Dan Sullivan asked what I was going to do when the industry took away all of my commissions. I told him that would never happen. And he said, no, it probably wouldn't, but did I know what I would do if it did? I didn't have an answer for him, and when I got back home I found I was really angry that he had asked the question. After a few days, I realized that I was upset because I knew I didn't have a contingency plan. I also knew that every year in the industry as a regulated advisor was becoming more frustrating and less satisfying, so maybe in the future it would become so intolerable that I would just quit, which would mean, in effect, that they had taken away my commissions! It was at that point that I got really serious about my Unique Process so I could create a future that didn't require commissions."

How advisors liberate or trap themselves.
Dan Taylor's experience is echoed by all the other Unique Process Advisors in this book. The crucial event in their professional careers came on the day that they clearly and consciously chose their clients over their commissions. Betty Norman remembers it as a commitment to personal integrity.

"Either the client's success and satisfaction is most important, or the commission for selling a product is most important: One or

Value Creation

Unique Process Advisors free themselves from dependancy on products by charging up front for a thinking-and-action process focused on the clients' most important D.O.S. (dangers, opportunities, and strengths) issues. Regardless of whether a product is utilized, the relationships are always well-paying and ongoing.

CLIENTS

THE CRUCIAL CHOICE

COMMISSIONS

Commoditization

Product-based advisors always depend upon the sale of commodities for their income. They must have many product sales as frequently as possible. With the best will in the world, advisors who are dependent only on products will favor their own financial self-interest over the strategic interests of the clients.

the other. And once you choose the client, it's amazing how liberated your thinking becomes. All of your client relationships blossom. But if you choose the products and commissions as your biggest priority, then, I believe, as an advisor, you become increasingly trapped, and your future starts to diminish."

All financial advisors are divided into two groups.
I've been coaching highly successful financial advisors since 1976. Over that time, I have had in-depth conversations with more than 2,000 individuals, each with at least 20 years of experience as an advisor. This equates to approximately 40,000 years of advisor experience in total. In all of those conversations, there is a central issue running down the middle of all this experience that divides all financial advisors into two distinct groups: On the one hand, we have the majority of advisors whose careers are controlled by the limitations and restrictions of the commoditized products they sell; and on the other, the minority who have liberated themselves by committing all of their wisdom and skills to transforming the lives and futures of their clientele.

Dependency: All the advisors featured in this book have taken the less-traveled but liberating path in their careers. They have been able to make this choice—clients over commissions—because they have built their businesses around a Unique Process. Without this continually evolving and transformative structure, they would not have been able to escape from the product-based dependency that characterizes the daily thinking and activities of the majority of advisors. This dependency shows up in three specific ways that are growing more onerous every year:

1. **Dependency on commoditization:** All "products" in the financial services industry, no matter how innovative, quickly become commoditized as soon as they enter the marketplace. If something is seen by competitors as successful,

they quickly and widely copy it. It is virtually impossible for advisors to achieve any kind of competitive advantage based on products. What is far more likely is that all product-based advisors will face increasing costs and complexity, and diminished profit margins, each successive year. Product-based advisors have no control over the design or performance of the commodities that they sell.

Unique Process Advisors, on the other hand, are able to create a Value Creation Monopoly with their clientele. Since the Unique Process is protected by intellectual property law, it cannot be copied without the advisor's permission. Inside of this monopoly advantage, business continually becomes simpler, more profitable, and more satisfying.

2. **Dependency on bureaucracy:** The commoditization of financial products always leads to the total bureaucratization of their manufacture and distribution. Product-based advisors have to contend more and more with the increasing complexities, complications, conflicts, and contradictions that invariably come from dealing with one or more large bureaucratic organizations. They are often at the mercy of bureaucratic processes, policies, and crises over which they have no control.

Unique Process Advisors lead lives and build businesses that are increasingly bureaucracy-free. Where they continue to sell financial products, they do so from a favored, advantageous position compared with other advisors. Bureaucracies come to them and compete for their business. Rob Darnbrough described the abrupt change in the treatment he received from head offices when it became obvious how successful his Unique Process was:

"They didn't exactly know what I was doing, but they knew it was different. They had a sense that I had a methodology

that was producing bigger results than the other agents out there. Before my Unique Process, I had to fight for their attention and service. Since I started using my process, they've had to fight for mine."

3. **Dependency on regulatory agencies:** The combination of commodities and bureaucracy attracts regulation, and that is doubly true when it involves large amounts of consumers' money. Financial advisors over the past two decades have faced increasing regulatory scrutiny and restrictions. What's ironic about this is that, while the worst and greatest examples of malfeasance in the financial industry have occurred at the bureaucratic level of large corporations, it is individual financial advisors who have been most penalized. This trend is likely to continue. Add to this the unpredictability: A great deal of what the regulators do seems arbitrary and capricious to the average advisor.

   Unique Process Advisors do not depend on regulatory sanction or approval to make a living. In fact, a growing number of Unique Process Advisors are relinquishing their industry licenses, enabling them to grow their entrepreneurial businesses in a regulation-free zone for the rest of their careers.

When Lee Brower speaks at meetings of product-based advisors, he often leaves them in stunned disbelief at the size of the fees that he charges for his Unique Process. But, as Lee points out, extraordinary fees only come when clients know that their lives are more important to you than your commissions are. We'll learn more about Lee's process, The Empowered Wealth System, in the following interview.

Lee Brower

The Empowered Wealth System™

Lee Brower, besides being an extraordinarily successful and articulate financial advisor, is both a client and an associate coach of the Strategic Coach Program. Over the past 20 years, he has specialized in bringing generational integration and teamwork to affluent families, enabling the families as unified communities to become positive contributors to society. Lee's Unique Process, which is called The Empowered Wealth System™, has been so effective that it is now being utilized as the core system for numerous professional advisors, businesses, educational institutions, and philanthropic organizations in the United States, Canada, and Mexico.

Dan Sullivan: Lee, I'm going to start this interview by asking you to reflect on some of the dangers you were experiencing as a financial advisor that led you to create The Empowered Wealth System.

Lee Brower: Ever since I was quite young, I had always felt there was great purpose to my life. So I think the overriding danger for me, Dan, was that I wasn't generating the results I felt gave me a feeling of purpose, and to live my life without finding that passion scared me. The other main thing is that I was seeing our industry and myself being caught up in the commodity business. And I had a much higher regard for my own wisdom than I had for all the commodities we were selling. We were very good at targeting products to the fear or greed of a client so we did a nice business, but everything was short term and repetitive and built around a commodity that our clients could purchase anywhere. I felt we were creating value because our clients were certainly better off. But our focus was exclusively centered on financial solutions, and what I observed was that most of our clients wanted more. The third main danger was that I was making ends meet and generating some short-term wealth, but it never seemed that I

was creating a whole lot for my future. So the idea that I could wake up three years later and have made no progress financially was very scary.

Dan Sullivan: When did you begin to reflect on the concept of Empowered Wealth?
Lee Brower: I can still remember the exact moment, Dan. It was at a time when I was working with a few very affluent families and beginning to develop some affluence myself. In a moment of reflection, this question came to me very vividly: "What is my stewardship responsibility to wealth, and when does it end?" I concluded that my financial wealth has no responsibility towards me, but I have a responsibility to it, and that responsibility never ends. It doesn't die when I do. It is ongoing.

Dan Sullivan: What exactly do you mean by stewardship to wealth? What does that entail?
Lee Brower: Well, so many people think that financial wealth is itself the end, but it is really only a means to an end. If you are a steward to your wealth, then you are employing your wealth in causes that are bigger than yourself. The individual health, happiness, and well-being of wealth creators is not dependent on how much money they have, but on how that money is responsibly employed in support of their passions.

Dan Sullivan: Could you talk a little about your definition of wealth, because I know for you wealth is much more than financial assets?
Lee Brower: We view wealth in the context of what we call The Quadrant Living System™. This system is based upon the findings of nearly three decades of research with affluent families. The basic premise is that when we ask affluent families if they possess assets more valuable than their financial assets, one hundred percent of the time they say yes. They respond with their family, their health, their heritage, their values, and so on. These are assets that they wouldn't trade for more money.

So we've separated an individual's or family's assets into four distinct quadrants: Financial Assets, Core Assets, Experience Assets, and Contribution Assets.

Dan Sullivan: Could you elaborate on each asset?
Lee Brower: Sure. Financial Assets are pretty self-explanatory: Financial Assets are those "things" identified on your financial balance sheet. Core Assets include your family, health, unique talents, heritage, and your intrinsic values or virtues. Experience Assets include education, wisdom from our good and bad experiences, our reputation, traditions, alliances, networks, and so forth. The last are Contribution Assets, and these are interesting. The government may define Contribution Assets as the money we must put back in society to do good. They call it "taxes." If you think about it, taxes do provide us with assets—roads, schools, protection, health care, defense, welfare, and so on. From an accounting sense, most people regard taxes as liabilities rather than assets. Why? Because it has become an obligation, and they have very little, if any, control over the employment of those taxes.

So, for us, Contribution Assets represent our gratitude assets. These are the money, time, talents, wisdom, and relationships allocated by the wealth creator to enrich society and causes dear to the family, where they don't have to give up choice and control over their assets. Now, when we present this system to the client, we ask them, "If you could transfer only three of these four asset categories to future generations, which one category would you leave behind?" Almost every time, they say that they would leave behind the Financial Assets because they know that if their heirs are rich in their Core, Experience, and Contribution Assets, the Financial Assets will take care of themselves.

Dan Sullivan: But they probably never focus on those other assets.
Lee Brower: We ask them where they've focused in their

> It's been said that only two percent of family wealth ever makes it past the third generation. So I think that's all you need to know about the effectiveness of traditional estate planning. And I'm saying this as somebody who has experienced it from the inside.

financial planning and estate planning, and, of course, for the great majority it is solely the Financial. And yet they had just told me that if they focus on the Core, Experience, and Contribution Assets, the Financial Assets will mature on their own. So the client has a powerful realization during this conversation that a different approach to true wealth planning is needed, and they become receptive to The Empowered Wealth System.

Dan Sullivan: You mentioned estate planning, Lee. I know you have very strong feelings about how estate planning is being done right now. Could you talk a little about that?

Lee Brower: If you look at the estate planning industry today, the basic strategy begins with identifying the number of heirs. Why? To divide the estate up amongst as many heirs as possible, utilizing all the gift and transfer techniques. One of the first rules of war is to "divide and conquer." And so, if I'm dividing the assets up, I'm setting that family up for failure. Our findings show that in all too many situations, traditional planning has done more to destroy families than taxes will ever do. Traditional estate planning operates around the four D's: Divide the assets, defer those assets downstream as far as possible, then dump them on what most times are the ill-prepared heirs, and watch those ultimately dissipate. It's been said that only two percent of family wealth ever makes it past the third generation. So I think that's all you need to know about the effectiveness of traditional estate planning.

Dan Sullivan: In this context, Lee, what are some of the major dangers facing the wealthy families you work with?

Lee Brower: Our research shows that most families are worried about going from a unified family that talks in terms of "we" to a divided family that talks in terms of "me" and "what's my share." One of the things wealth creators are most proud of is that they are contributors to society: They create jobs, they create revenue, and they create opportunities. And one of their fears is that their children or their grandchildren could end up just the opposite, as takers from society. Most families have these fears, but they operate on a very reactive basis. They wait for conflict to happen and then try to settle it. The Empowered Wealth/Quadrant Living System creates systems that can help the children and grandchildren be stewards to their wealth and behave like first-generation wealth creators, with all four quadrants balanced.

Dan Sullivan: Because of the dangers these families face and their inability to act on them in a creative way, what are some of the real negative results you have seen?

Lee Brower: I've seen tragedy after tragedy—family businesses absolutely destroyed. Regardless of the current status of a family, part of our mission is to get every family member to agree on "family first" and "together we are better." If we can get everyone to sign off on just that, then we have the potential to build a virtual family cooperative that is building and reinforcing all the quadrants of true wealth.

> The Empowered Wealth/ Quadrant Living System creates systems that can help the children and grandchildren be stewards to their wealth and behave like first-generation wealth creators ...

Dan Sullivan: Now, Lee, I think this is a good time to talk about the stages of your Unique Process. How do you approach these situations when you're called in as a consultant?

Lee Brower: We have four stages to our process, and the four stages are the same regardless of the current condition of the family. The initial stage is what we call The Location and Vision Experience™. "Where are you now and where do you want to be?" We ask the families to reflect on their wealth in the context of the four quadrants. They go through the Clarity Experience that clearly identifies the collective vision of the family. We identify loose ends in their planning that do not match their vision. The family is very clear what assets and liabilities they have in each of the four quadrants. We spend more time here than we do in the other stages because we know if we get the initial conditions right, we will have dramatically increased our potential for success with this family. We charge a fee for that assessment process and we have, you know, significant deliverables that come along with it. The next stage is The Quadrant Living Solution™. This is the Design and Build Stage. A blueprint is created that matches the objectives of the family, and we identify The Empowered Wealth Design Team™. These are the professionals who will be involved in the design of the plan. They may include specialists in law, accounting, tax, philanthropy, and even psychology. The client then signs off on the steps that need to be completed. This leads to The Solution Empowerment™, which is the building stage. This is where we actually implement the design that enables the family to achieve their goals and objectives. We conclude this stage with The Empowered Family Retreat™.

Dan Sullivan: What is the final stage?
Lee Brower: The final stage is The Perpetual Confidence Extender™. And this is basically our model for how to maintain confidence and balance in our clients' lives. The first criterion is attentiveness because to maintain positive results for the long term, we need to make sure the family is continually attending to the four quadrants. The other aspect is accountability. Because these families have legions of advisors, we feel it's important to hold regular accountability meetings with all

their advisors. In these meetings, we ask the advisors to reflect on three questions: "What have I done to create value for this family over the last 12 months?" "What do I intend to do to create value for this family over the next 12 months?" And, "What makes me unique, and why should the family continue to do business with me?" Knowing that you have to answer these three questions every year takes all the advisors, including me, from a reactive realm to a proactive realm. So with this process, we are not only able to address short-term objectives the family may have, we also create a positive framework for building a multigenerational productive family.

Dan Sullivan: Talk a little about the Family Bank concept as it relates to this process.

Lee Brower: The Family Quadrant Empowered Bank™ is a concept, not a chartered financial institution. It is the glue that holds the quadrants together and provides the efficient interaction among those quadrants within the family. A tremendous amount of time is devoted to establishing and honing the family governance. By having a system in place to pre-empt dangers and to reinforce the strengths of the family, the opportunities for the family increase and their confidence soars. They truly become a high-impact family of high-impact individuals.

> By having a system in place to pre-empt dangers and to reinforce the strengths of the family, the opportunities for the family increase and their confidence soars. They truly become a high-impact family of high-impact individuals.

Dan Sullivan: What is your target audience for The Empowered Wealth System?

Lee Brower: Well, there are really two sides to that question: What is the best target audience for our team financially, and what is the best target audience to employ the system we are supporting? When we first started out, we believed our process was best suited for families with a net worth that exceeded $25 million, and this is the level of many of our families. But we have also determined that financial cutoffs are not the best policy. So what we really look for are families with an active and growing net worth who have a cause bigger than themselves. Now, we did an experiment a few summers ago where we went out and shared The Quadrant Living System with an audience with a median net worth of $150,000. The response was overwhelming—70 percent of the audience was so impressed that they emailed us saying these principles were already changing their lives. We have since created a Quadrant Living Lite that applies to all families, regardless of net worth. When you're dealing with true principles, true principles help everyone.

Dan Sullivan: One of my theories about financial advisors in the 21st century is that they will constantly create new social, political, and economic forms. You've clearly done that, Lee, with The Quadrant Living System approach, so could you talk about your relationship with education?

Lee Brower: Our value creation model here is serving as a model to help universities produce what we call "high-impact humans." We are currently working with two universities utilizing the quadrants as a model to identify the result of each class being offered. The idea is that students who are taught how to employ all four quadrants (Core, Experience, Contribution, and Financial) become high-impact individuals. Our role is also to help the university identify the leading indicators of students who will succeed in school, graduate on time, and give back. I believe there can be a very powerful, synergistic relationship because by introducing this system through universities, we are simultaneously introducing it to affluent alumni.

Dan Sullivan: Looking ten or twenty years down the line, where do you see these collaborations going?

Lee Brower: First, in a survey we did with affluent families, they told us that the number one need they were not getting and did not know how to get was education for their children. Not traditional education, but, really, education related to all the quadrants. So we've made this our initiative. We'll create an environment where experiential learning can take place for heirs of affluence. Every affluent parent wishes they could give their children the experiences that made them successful. They can't. However, experiential learning through games and other experiences is the next best thing. If I look ahead, my 25-year plan is that Empowered Wealth/Quadrant Living will have its own campus location where we can hold seminars and utilize technology to process and disseminate information to all families about what other families are doing, what's working, and so on. I also see political leaders and corporate leaders coming to the Empowered Wealth/Quadrant Living campus to discuss programs and major initiatives. So if the president of a country wants to attract U.S. investors, he could come to the Empowered Wealth/Quadrant Living campus and discuss the four quadrants and how that investment would be put to use not only as a financial improvement, but as an investment in the Core, Experience, and Contribution Assets as well.

Dan Sullivan: Let's talk about industry transformation, Lee. Do you see your process as a career path for other advisors?
Lee Brower: Definitely. We realize that there is a huge need, and we really want to make the process work for them. We have an association of advisors who come together frequently for sharing and training. We recently held a "boot camp" with over 40 advisors in attendance. We're trying to make the process more standardized and take care of some licensing issues, but we're excited about how it's progressing.

Dan Sullivan: What kind of advisor from an experience standpoint and a success standpoint is in the best position to take advantage of this?

Lee Brower: We have a membership program where advisors can select their area of interest and expertise. I think that professional advisors generating net revenue in excess of a half-million dollars a year who have a quality client base are best suited for becoming Quadrant Living Architects. They need to be in relationships where they are serving as advisors and not tactical sales people. Others can utilize the training to become Quadrant Living Specialists using Quadrant training to optimize their area of specialty.

Dan Sullivan: What are some of the results you've seen from advisors who have implemented the system?
Lee Brower: Well, The Quadrant Living System will open doors to relationships that have never been open before. I was just talking to one of our Quadrant Living Architects who used the Quadrant Living System to attract a client whose family is worth $600 million. After one meeting that client was raving about the process and saying, "I wish I had seen this 20 years ago when I did my estate planning, and I am going to do everything possible to implement this now." Usually somebody that wealthy will have dozens of paid advisors, and you usually don't get that type of response after the first visit. And I would say that up until then, the largest client that particular advisor had ever worked with was in the $15 million to $20 million range. So he was able to go out and engage a client worth $600 million.

Dan Sullivan: It's exciting to see you evolve into your role as a Unique Process Advisor, Lee, because I've known you for many years. You've been in the Strategic Coach Program since 1995, so could you reflect on the role the Coach has played over the last 13 years?
Lee Brower: Sure. When I first entered Strategic Coach, I had a lot of messes in my life. I was going through an IRS audit, I had employees I wasn't happy with, I was selling some businesses, I was, you know, bogged down in the minutiae. And I kept thinking, "How in the world am I going to get ahead?" So what

Strategic Coach gave me were systems to clean up those messes, and the tools to develop my own systems. These were tools that really allowed me to build a life around my passions, my goals, my personality—and make huge progress. My gratitude towards Strategic Coach is just overwhelming. And it's really just beginning because each year Strategic Coach becomes more and more prevalent in my life.

Dan Sullivan: One of the things that strikes me, Lee, is that the principles you've developed not only guide your financial advising, but your entire lifestyle and world view. Would you agree?

Lee Brower: There is no doubt that by living Empowered Wealth/Quadrant Living principles, I am a better leader in my home and in my business. Our family has a common vision, with systems to help each of us become contributors to society and not just takers. It has without question made us better.

Dan Sullivan: To conclude, why don't you talk a little about your emotional outlook as an advisor.

Lee Brower: Well, I just have more confidence than at any time in my career. I have the confidence to say no when something is interfering with success. I'm not afraid to bring in other people and delegate around my Unique Ability®. When I meet with people now, I don't care who they are or what their status is. I have a very calm demeanor because I have immense confidence in my ability to create value around the Wealth Empowerment principles. When I first started this journey, I had a lot of dangers and instabilities, but today I am at once excited and at peace with my path as an advisor and a continuous creator of intellectual capital.

For contact details on The Empowered Wealth System, please see page 231.

IDEA 4

The Power Of Transformative Conversations

"Something magical happens when a conversation is open-ended, and people can discover their own crucial insights and breakthroughs. When it's their insight, when it's their break-through, they become passion-ately committed to it."

The Power Of Transformative Conversations

Escaping from The Commoditization Trap*.

Tom Miller is passionate about conversations. This comes from his belief that clients only truly commit themselves to solutions they discover from their own thinking. But not just any thinking. The thinking that leads to strategic break-throughs can only be experienced within an in-depth, multi-dimensional conversation with a financial advisor who is truly client-focused. Here's what Tom has discovered from working within his own Unique Process:

"There are certain kinds of thoughts, decisions, and actions that people can't get to unless they are able to have a great con-versation with somebody they respect and trust. Something magical happens when a conversation is open-ended, and people can discover their own crucial insights and break-throughs. When it's their insight, when it's their breakthrough, they become passionately committed to it. Otherwise, they're just taking in more information on top of all the information that's already overwhelming them. People today don't want any more information. What they want are great conversations that enable them to make great decisions."

Unique Processes™ are designed to create great conversations.
Though all Unique Processes are different, they are all the same in that they are designed to create extraordinary conversations between advisors and their clients. Tom Miller's VisionLink

*For the definition of The Commoditization Trap, please see page 228.

- In-depth, multi-dimensional, and client-focused.

- Integrates and focuses advisor wisdom and client issues.

- Profoundly different from product-based "sales tracks."

- Unique Process pays the advisor to have great conversations.

- Advisor and client escape from being commoditized.

- Rare experience that clients have never had before.

- Both advisor and client are protected by the process.

- From adversarial to a partnership relationship.

process is focused on creating compensation programs for successful companies and corporations. This process integrates the wisdom that Tom has developed over 20 years of working with hundreds of successful companies, combined with his in-depth understanding of business development and growth. All of this is unique to Tom and his team. No other financial advisor or company in the industry has an approach that resembles VisionLink. Most of what Tom provides to his clientele is proprietary.

Profoundly different: But at the bottom of the VisionLink process is an extraordinary conversation. And this is also true for all the other advisors featured in this book. When I interviewed each of them, they all said that the secret to why their processes worked so well lay in the power of the extraordinary conversations that were generated. They also said that these conversations were profoundly different from talks they had had with clientele when they were still trying to sell products. Debra Schatzki talks about how enjoyable it is to have everything be about conversations:

"I never had conversations like this when I was trying to sell insurance. The biggest reason, quite frankly, was because I wasn't paid to have great conversations. But I am paid to do my process, and because the client has already paid for my time, and my wisdom, and my creativity, I provide as much as I possibly can."

Just the opposite of the commoditization experience.
In their book, *The Support Economy*, Shoshana Zuboff and James Maxmin write that there is a growing consumer revolt in all industries against the experience of being commoditized in the sales process. Financial corporations for the most part have not responded creatively or well to this trend. Many of them have increased the level of commoditization in their product and service offerings. They continue to strip away everything that is personal and unique from their approach. This is a great opportunity, then, for those advisors who

approach their clientele from within a Unique Process. The moment that clients and customers enter into the process, they immediately sense that they're being dealt with uniquely. This is just the opposite of being commoditized.

Rare experience: Mary Anne Ehlert feels the conversations that result from her Unique Process are different because, from start to finish, they are totally focused on the client and the client's issues:

"The other person knows, from the first moment, that they have my complete and undivided attention. Immediately, they know that this is a rare experience because they don't get this from anyone else. My Unique Process is about them; it isn't about me. The moment they enter the first stage of the process, they sense they are in a very safe environment that's designed just for them. Where else have they experienced that?"

Protection for both the client and the advisor.
Mary Anne's description of the "safe environment" jibes with the experiences of other Unique Process Advisors. The safety applies two ways. Certainly, the clients feel that they are being listened to. And for many of them, that's unique in their experience of dealing with financial advisors. The Unique Process ensures that clients are provided with the advisor's best and most committed attention, on the one hand, and it ensures that advisors are well compensated for providing this attention, on the other. Within the Unique Process, this best and most committed attention occurs all of the time, every time.

A communicative, cooperative, and creative partnership.
As a result, both clients and advisors are able to be at their most communicative, cooperative, and creative. They become partners in creating much bigger, better, and more enjoyable futures for each other. The Unique Process is the protective structure that enables this partnership to be established and

to flourish. Rob Darnbrough says that his Unique Process enabled him, for the first time, to sit "on the other side of the table" with his clients:

"I think, traditionally in the financial industry, there has always been an adversarial relationship between advisors and their clients. That's because of the commissions on product sales. In the back of their minds, or maybe in the front of their minds, the clients always knew everything was being done to get them to buy a product so the advisor could get a commission. So even in the best relationships, they always had their guard up. But the moment they enter my Unique Process, their guard goes down because they know my agenda isn't about a product. They've already paid me up front to help clarify their thoughts and put together a gameplan based on their priorities. This allows me to be a partner on their side of the table. It's a much better way to live your life as an advisor."

Scott Keffer has built his Donor Motivation Program entirely on the power of transformative conversations. He observed that in most philanthropic organizations, their discussions with prospective donors are self-serving and boring. Let's learn how he solves this problem.

Scott Keffer
The Donor Motivation Program™

Scott Keffer, a long-time participant in Strategic Coach, has created a Unique Process called The Donor Motivation Program, focused on the philanthropic planning sector. As has been the case with all of our Unique Process Advisors, Scott immediately communicates an enormous passion for the new kind of value he is creating in the marketplace. And, as has also been the case with the others, he not only uses his Unique Process to enable his direct clients to transform their situations, he has designed and packaged The Donor Motivation Program™ as a new ready-to-use capability that allows other financial and estate planning advisors to work more successfully with their own clients in the philanthropic field.

Dan Sullivan: Scott, this interview is designed to showcase innovative advisors who have reinvented themselves as Unique Process Advisors. I want to emphasize to our readers, many of whom are worried and frustrated by their career path, that change always begins through a process of deep reflection by advisors who are committed to achieving a future bigger than their past. Could you talk a little about the origins of The Donor Motivation Program and the process through which this idea crystallized?

Scott Keffer: In 1994, I had been in the financial services industry for about 15 years. The first five were in retail, developing my own clients. The next ten were focused on essentially a support role, a wholesale role, helping financial advisors, money managers, and insurance agents better serve their affluent clients. This role led me into advanced estate planning, which is where I discovered the power of philanthropic planning.

Dan Sullivan: But then you went back into retail.
Scott Keffer: Yes. I don't know if I lost my mind or found it, but I decided to go back into retail. I wanted to establish a practice that would help affluent individuals leave a lasting legacy by integrating philanthropy into their wealth planning. My biggest problems were having no client relationships and no credibility or exposure in the community—not to mention that every advisor is after the affluent. So I decided to approach charities directly. I essentially said, "Here's who I am. Here is my planning process. Why don't you introduce me to your affluent donors?"

Dan Sullivan: Were the charities receptive?
Scott Keffer: No. I struck out over and over again. The charities had heard that proposition many, many times before. I finally realized that I was trying to market myself, not bring value to the charities. In fact, I was asking them to expose me to their biggest asset, their highly affluent donors.

Dan Sullivan: Now, throughout this period, you were attending Strategic Coach sessions.
Scott Keffer: Yes. The Strategic Coach sessions compelled me to continually focus on developing a value proposition. So I asked myself this question, "What would charities pay me to do for them?" At the time, I was also reading *The 22 Immutable Laws of Marketing*. The Law of Category says that if you are not first in a brand line, then create a new line and become first in it.

Dan Sullivan: Why did you zero in on donor motivation?
Scott Keffer: At the time, one of the other concepts the Coach sessions were focusing us on was Unique Ability®, and mine was in the area of communication, specifically motivation. I realized that I could provide value by creating a program to motivate donors to want to have a planned-giving conversation with charities.

Dan Sullivan: So your value proposition is centered on donor motivation.

Scott Keffer: Right. Initially, it was basically just a donor seminar that I would present four times a year. To determine if the concept had value, I ran it by the director of development for the United Way here in Pittsburgh. He made a number of good suggestions and then hired me, as did three other charities, in 1995. That was really the dawn of The Donor Motivation Program.

Dan Sullivan: For the benefit of our readers who are hearing about this for the first time, why don't you outline step by step your Donor Motivation Program?
Scott Keffer: Sure. Our process for donor motivation has three stages: one, attract qualified donors; two, motivate them to a conversation; and, three, nurture them to a future decision. The main tool in Stage 1 is called The Donor Sequential Invitation System™. Once we got the seminars going, we realized that one of the biggest problems most charities face is getting donors into the room. And so we created a sequential invitation system that has donor-tested pieces for attracting donors to the event in accordance with a carefully laid out invitation timeline.

Central to the invitation process is donor targeting: Charities don't simply want to get people in the room, they want to get the right people in the room. We use an ABC system to help charities categorize and target their best donors: An "A" donor is a major giver, well known to the charity; a "B" donor is somebody who gives consistently; a "C" donor is somebody who has given anything over the past five years. Research shows that the biggest opportunities in charitable giving are among the B and C donors because they're the "millionaire next door"—and many of them don't show up on the radar screen when charities use socio-economic screens to find them. So we created an invitation system that allows a charity to cost effectively attract qualified donors from their entire donor base.

The tool in the second stage we call The Donor Action Capture Process™. That process begins with a world-class seminar experience. Many charities misunderstand the purpose of the seminar. They believe it is to "sell" or get a decision about a planned gift. Therefore, they typically put on technical seminars—which they believe will help a donor make a decision about a planned gift. In actuality, technical seminars confuse donors. Decisions about planned gifts are not made at seminars, or on websites, or by reading brochures or articles or mail pieces. The decision to complete a planned gift happens in one place only—in conversation with a professional.

> The real focus of the presentation is to facilitate powerful communication — to get donors in a position where they are excited about starting a conversation with a professional.

So what we provide is a fool-proof system to conduct a world-class Front Stage experience for the donor, where we take a complex subject and make it simple for them to understand. Sure, we get into some financial discussions, the implications for tax planning, and so on. The real focus of the presentation is to facilitate powerful communication—to get donors in a position where they are excited about starting a conversation with a professional. Once we've completed The C² Donor Presentation and the donors in the room feel empowered to move ahead, The Donor Action Capture Process gives each donor a menu of options to take action. The action is always a conversation with someone—their current advisor, the planned giving professional from the charity, or the presenter, which is either me or one of our licensees.

Finally, in Stage 3, we nurture those who don't take action at the event to future decision through the The Donor Nurture Process™. In this stage, we recognize that it takes between 18 and 24 interactions before the majority of people make a decision.

This is where we water the seeds, so to speak, that have been planted at the event through a series of powerful communication pieces. Then, three months later, we invite them to the next event, and the systematic process begins all over again: attract, motivate, nurture.

Dan Sullivan: Talk a little about The D.O.S. Conversation*, Scott, because I know it figures very prominently in this process.
Scott Keffer: Well, The D.O.S. Conversation® has become the laboratory, if you will, of our innovation. Every stage of the process is constructed around the dangers, opportunities, and strengths of the donors and the charities. So, for example, a large frustration for many charities is getting the right donors to hear the powerful message we've created. Therefore, the invitations and phone scripts are carefully crafted and targeted around the dangers, opportunities, and strengths of donors; they really speak directly to the donor's inner sanctum and create maximum responsiveness. When charities ask about the secret of our success, I like to tell them that "we speak 'donor.'" All that means is that we continually speak to the D.O.S. of the donors. The reason our Unique Process is so effective is because it simplifies a complex, often arcane subject, and we achieve this discipline throughout our process by focusing our message around The D.O.S Conversation. Finally, as a communication template, The D.O.S. Conversation is really invaluable because it sets the parameters for powerful dialogue between the charities and donors.

> When charities ask about the secret of our success, I like to tell them that "we speak 'donor.'"

Dan Sullivan: It strikes me that your use of The D.O.S. Conversation is a particularly effective strategy for addressing the challenge of reaching baby boom donors who may be new to the planned giving process.

*For the definition of The D.O.S. Conversation, please see page 229.

Scott Keffer: That's a great point, Dan. This baby boom generation is really rewriting the charitable giving landscape, just as they redefined the coffee, the computer, the car, the electronics industries. Fidelity Gift Fund went from nothing in 1992 to the number one grant-making charity in the country in six short years. They did it because they paid attention to the baby boom generation and gave them what they wanted: control, options, and flexibility. Baby boomers need to reposition assets to create lifetime income, and then they are open to the idea of leaving a legacy. Planned giving tools are the perfect solution to their needs.

Dan Sullivan: Well, whether they're a baby boomer or not, I think what donors increasingly demand is an informative, exciting Front Stage experience from the charity. In the Strategic Coach Program, we make a very careful distinction between the "Front Stage" and "Back Stage" of an organization. Talk a little about how your Donor Motivation Program serves as both the Front Stage and Back Stage provider for these charities.

Scott Keffer: The Front Stage/Back Stage Model™* had a very powerful influence on our development of the program and continues to drive our innovation. I like to use the Disney Institute as an example. If you ask them who Disney's competition is, they don't cite Six Flags, Universal, and all the other amusement parks. Rather, they say, "No, our competition is FedEx, Starbucks, Canyon Ranch, and Four Seasons." Because from Disney's perspective, the service offering that guests experience in any arena becomes the standard they compare all service offerings to, and the same is true for my company. Many of the donors we work with are high-net-worth individuals who expect the "Four Seasons" of donor presentations, and we give them a world-class Front Stage experience. But we also provide the charities with a whole set of Back Stage services to foolproof the "Four Seasons" Front Stage experience. So when they buy The Donor Motivation Program, they're really buying the total package, a complete turnkey

*For the definition of The Front Stage/Back Stage Model, please see page 229.

system. They can open it up, and batteries are included. It has been referred to, in a good way, as "donor motivation for dummies."

> To date, over 40 leading charities have been happy to pay me because my value creation model is so refreshing to planned giving specialists who are used to a financial services industry that only extracts value.

Dan Sullivan: This is really a phenomenal process, Scott, because you've totally transformed the relationship between financial and estate planning advisors and charitable organizations. As you've said, most advisors are going to these charities and not creating value for the charity, but actually asking the charity to create value for them by exposing them to affluent donors. So you've really transformed the entire relationship between advisors and charities into a value creation relationship.

Scott Keffer: That's right. And we take it one step further by guaranteeing each and every charity's satisfaction. We've really turned the tables on the industry, and I've used our value creation model to disempower the competition because most advisors are in there only trying to create value for themselves.

Dan Sullivan: You've also transformed the relationship between advisors and charities by charging a fee for services that many advisors provide for free, so talk a little about this decision.

Scott Keffer: It was really scary initially to ask for a fee to do something that I was trained to believe I should do for free. I can really credit Strategic Coach for building my confidence and changing my mindset. To date, over 40 leading charities have been happy to pay me because my value creation model is so refreshing to planned giving specialists who are used to a financial services industry that only extracts value.

Dan Sullivan: Scott, we are well into this conversation, and you haven't yet mentioned a financial services product or company. What's wrong with you?

Scott Keffer: You've successfully changed my thinking, Dan. We still have our core wealth planning business based on fees and product sales. However, The Donor Motivation Program is not about products, but about bringing value to the charity and their donors. Sure, at the presentations we talk about tax planning and a three-dimensional concept of wealth—financial, personal, and social—but the focus is on the donors' D.O.S. rather than selling products or promoting the charity. We begin each presentation by telling the donors that "this may be the only charitable event you come to where there's nothing to buy, nowhere to write a check. Take your hands off your wallet and relax."

It is liberating and refreshing for the donors to attend an event that is all about them and their concerns—the things that cause them to lose sleep.

Dan Sullivan: Well, you've made the same transition away from product that all our featured Unique Process Advisors have undergone. And I think what's striking about your case, Scott, is that you've really become a resource, not only to individual clients, but to the entire planned giving community.

Scott Keffer: This gets back to The D.O.S. Conversation, Dan, because I really think that we hold a lot of insight into the dangers, opportunities, and strengths of the planned giving industry. And that has allowed us to become, as you say, a resource to the community. In the fall of 2003, for example, I hosted The Charitable Leaders Forum for 20 select planned giving professionals. Here, we had sort of a fact-finding session centered around the D.O.S., the dangers and obstacles, in the planned giving community. After the conference, my staff and I created a white paper, eventually transferred into a PowerPoint presentation, entitled "The Six Disturbing Trends and Challenges that Threaten Business as Usual for Charitable Fund Raisers."

Dan Sullivan: What did you do with the white paper?

Scott Keffer: That spring, we invited 100 planned giving professionals, and over 75 showed up, to hear the results of our research. A third of them actually asked to have the report delivered to their board members, advisory committees, or directors of development. So it was a really powerful communication piece that reached the highest levels of many charities. We continue to update the report annually and deliver it regularly across the country. What we have found is that, like most industries, much of the planned giving community is truly unaware of their own dangers and opportunities. Much of our credibility and value as a resource is really in educating them about their D.O.S.

Dan Sullivan: Could you boil down the essence of the value proposition to the charities?

Scott Keffer: Sure. One of the biggest issues for a charity is securing their financial future and reducing the stress that current fundraising causes. The best method to do this is through building endowment, and one of the best methods for building endowment is to grow planned giving. The biggest obstacle to growing planned giving is finding and motivating key donors. The Donor Motivation Program is the most cost-effective and time-efficient system for charities to systematically and continuously grow planned giving. That is why the finest charities in our community are willing to hire us and pay us a fee. We recently launched The Donor Motivation Institute, which we hope will one day be the preeminent source of research on donor motivation.

Dan Sullivan: You're not only a resource to the planned giving community, Scott, but also to other financial and estate planning advisors. As is the case with every one of our Unique Process Advisors, you're allowing other advisors to transform themselves through an exciting Unique Process. Talk about your efforts to empower other advisors to adopt The Donor Motivation Program.

Scott Keffer: In 2003, we began licensing our system to financial advisors who, like me, had always wanted to work with charities but failed. One advisor in New Jersey had struck out at 60 charities before our program, but ultimately signed up six of those charities to The Donor Motivation Program. Our program continues to impact his business by positioning him as the "go-to" firm in his community and allowing him to get paid to educate leaders in his community.

Dan Sullivan: Scott, what has been the biggest challenge in terms of helping other advisors become successful with your program?
Scott Keffer: The biggest challenge was to create a complete process that could be easily integrated into their current business model. The process must enable the licensed advisor to sign a charity, to service the charity by staging the events, and to meet with interested donors. So, we had to create a marketing system that would accomplish three things for our advisors. First, it had to reposition the advisor as a resource to the charity. Next, it had to be an efficient system that would attract the very best charities. Finally, it had to be a turnkey marketing system that could be operated by their team. The result is our Just Sign One Auto Marketing System. It literally draws the right charities to the advisor's office to hear the special report. The system is operated by the team, and all the advisor needs to do is "show up and sing."

At the end of the report, the charity can sign up to have their current planned giving program analyzed by the advisor. That way, the advisor is invited in as a consultant and not a salesperson. The marketing system works day and night, automatically positioning the advisor as a resource to the local charities. Once they get hired, The Just Serve One System allows the advisor's team to support the charity and stage four world-class donor events per year. At the event, the advisor is being paid to educate the very people that he or she would like to meet—affluent donors of major charities. During the presentation, the charity is positioning the advisor as an expert and offering each donor an opportunity to have a one-hour conversation with the advisor.

At the event, the advisor is being paid to educate the very people that he or she would like to meet—affluent donors to major charities.

Dan Sullivan: What has been most rewarding for you?

Scott Keffer: It's very satisfying, Dan, to see other advisors who want to integrate philanthropic planning transform their practices by allowing them to meet affluent, influential people in their community on a preferred basis. Interestingly, our program has been successful not only here in the United States, but in Canada as well. Even though Canada's estate tax laws are different, the issues and the needs are the same for the charities, for the donors, and for the advisors. In addition, we began licensing estate planning attorneys, who are having phenomenal success. It's very satisfying for our team to see advisors grow and transform their practices systematically, relentlessly, and automatically. We're helping to close the "giving gap" that exists between affluent individuals, the charities, and the advisors who want to serve them both.

Dan Sullivan: Scott, let's talk about results a bit, because I know our readers and other advisors who may be contemplating adopting this process want to make sure their bottom line is protected. What's the impact on your planning business?

Scott Keffer: It's important to understand that this program works because it's not about marketing me; it's about serving the charity and bringing them value. By my serving them, the charities become my "credibility partner"—positioning me in the community as an expert. Since 1995, I've had over 10,000 donors attend my presentations. As you can imagine, this type of exposure has had a profound effect on my core wealth planning business. Affluent individuals cannot be chased; they must be attracted. This process makes me, and our licensees, very attractive to the affluent.

Dan Sullivan: Final question: Let's say Scott Keffer didn't go in this direction but just continued to be a financial advisor selling product. Where would he be, given the state of the financial services industry today?

Scott Keffer: I would not have been able to build a core philanthropic estate planning business from scratch that is focused solely on the affluent. I would have been forced to take the traditional route, selling products to lower-level clients, with all the fears and insecurities associated with that. Instead, I am impacting the charities in a very positive way. That is very fulfilling. In a broader sense, I really feel confident that by mastering The D.O.S. Conversation, I can create value for anyone, anywhere—I can change industries in effect. So that realization has been incredibly liberating to me, because regardless of the macro trends in the financial services industry, I know that I can create value and prosper as a Unique Process Advisor.

For contact details on The Donor Motivation Program, please see page 232.

IDEA 5

Asking About Everything

"That's the great breakthrough that the Unique Process has provided. It's a protective structure that encourages discovery of client issues at the deepest possible level. It's much more enjoyable to get paid up front to be the best possible advisor."

Idea 5

Asking About Everything

Talking about what clients want to talk about.

All the advisors in this book agree that their Unique Process produces much deeper conversations with clientele. They contrast this experience with earlier periods in their careers when they focused on selling insurance and investment products. Betty Norman, especially, found the product-based approach both deficient and unsatisfying:

"For most of my adult life prior to becoming an advisor, I had been involved in counseling and coaching of one kind or another. When I entered financial services, I was a bit appalled by how superficial the sales approaches were. But since then, I've learned that if you put the emphasis on selling a financial product, you are encouraged to make the sale happen as fast as possible—which means it's going to be shallow. As a result, the clients are left with a kind of empty feeling."

Betty reports that since she transformed her financial practice into a Unique Process, she gets rewarded for being a "deep listener," and her clients love the experience of identifying their most important concerns.

The Unique Process finances deep, satisfying conversations.
Charlie Epstein reports that his desire to get more deeply into his clients' problems and opportunities actually forced him to develop his Unique Process:

"I wanted to get rewarded for the quality of the conversations

Deep, wide, and big

The questions that are asked within a Unique Process lead to conversations that are comprehensive, insightful, strategic, and transformative for both advisor and client.

ASK ABOUT EVERYTHING

ASK AS LITTLE AS POSSIBLE

Shallow, narrow, and small

Questions asked within a product-based sales track tend to be superficial, dealing only with those client issues that support the fastest possible transaction.

I was having, and I wanted the money up front so I could forget about the product sale. That's why having a Unique Process is so crucial. It finances the ability to have the deepest, most expansive conversations."

Charlie agrees with Betty Norman that having a product-focused emphasis practically guarantees you won't have a conversation that leads to the best solutions:

"The way we were trained to sell products was to tell the clients what they want and need. Ignore anything they say that doesn't lead directly and quickly to the sale. So you never get deep. You never find out what really worries and motivates them. And here's a truth I've discovered that really matters: The deeper the issues you uncover are, the more powerful the solutions you create will be, and the more the client becomes a lifetime fan."

Advisors get to ask and talk about everything.
I remember speaking to a conference of Top of the Table insurance agents in 1993. One of the agents at my session asked me why I was so interested in his industry. I told him that financial advisors were fascinating to me because they were the only profession in the world that "got to ask about everything." This caused a big stir in the room and a lot of head-nodding. But I added that advisors would never ask the best possible questions if they weren't paid for doing it in every prospect and client relationship.

Going where the clients want to go.
Lee Brower says that his interest in having great conversations with his clients took a quantum leap the moment he started charging for his Unique Process:

"The companies and the industry associations always tell you that you have to put aside your self-interest, but the fact is you're

not paid to do that. All of the financial incentives are geared to looking after the company's interests and your own self-interests first. It wasn't until I received my first check for my process that I felt totally encouraged to go anywhere the clients wanted to go in the conversation. Once that kind of open-ended approach happened for the first time, and I was paid to do it, my passion for deep conversations increased exponentially."

Over the years, I have talked to industry executives about the importance of open-ended conversations. Many of them seemed not to understand what I was talking about. The whole idea of allowing clients and customers to direct the conversation was opposed to everything they believed in. Other executives thought it was a good idea in theory, but, "of course, we have to sell as much product as possible." And, of course, that's the truth. If the main priority is the greatest number of product sales, then what clients want will always be of less interest.

A protective structure for the best possible discoveries.
Tom Miller says that when his business was based on selling products, he always felt that the clock was ticking against him. The longer into a conversation he went with his clients, the more he had the feeling that he was paying for it out of his own pocket:

"I try to be an honorable person, dedicated to the clients' best interests. I've always done that. But before I had my Unique Process to actually pay me for being honorable and dedicated, the experience of selling products caused me a lot of anxiety. That's the great breakthrough that the Unique Process has provided. It's a protective structure that encourages discovery of client issues at the deepest possible level. It's much more enjoyable to get paid up front to be the best possible advisor."

When I talk to the best advisors in the industry, they all voice sentiments similar to Tom's. They want to be both virtuous and successful, and get paid continually for improving both their internal qualities and their external achievements.

The irony is that twice as much product gets sold.
One of the things that surprised all the Unique Process Advisors was that by focusing entirely on the clients' issues, they were able to sell far more product at the end of the process. Most felt that their product sales had at least doubled. Sometimes the increase was much more than that. Dan Taylor commented on this delightful outcome:

"Because I wasn't putting any emphasis on product sales, when it came time to use the product, the clients told me to do whatever was necessary. Since our conversations as a result of my Unique Process had taken all of their issues into account, it called for much bigger solutions. So the insurance coverage was much higher. And since they now saw me as a coach and counselor they could depend on for the long run, they gave me all their money to invest. Not only did I get paid up front, my payment at the end was much bigger."

Debra Schatzki will tell you that she likes to talk, and she likes to ask about everything. What she realized, however, was that few financial advisors and accountants feel comfortable talking outside of a very narrow spectrum of topics. She also observed that it is usually difficult for advisors and accountants to cooperate with each other because they don't speak the same language. Her Financial Services In A Box process transforms the teamwork between these two professions in such a way that they have more comprehensive conversations with clients. We learn more about Debra's Unique Process in the interview that follows.

Debra Schatzki
Financial Services In A Box™

In this interview, I'm pleased to introduce Debra Schatzki, a very successful financial services entrepreneur and a long-time participant in the Strategic Coach Program. Like all of the previous Unique Process Advisors I've talked with in this book, Debra has created a marvelous Unique Process — Financial Services In A Box™ — that solves a fundamental problem in the marketplace. In this case, how can accounting firms and financial advisors successfully integrate their wisdom to increase the value that's being created for their clients? From the success she has experienced using her process to solve this industry-wide problem, Debra realized that she had created a template that other financial services professionals could utilize in their practices.

Dan Sullivan: Let's start with some background, Debra, because it's important that our readers understand the origins of your process. When did you first begin to focus on the great, unrealized possibilities for cooperation between financial advisors and accounting firms?
Debra Schatzki: Well, I was in a family financial services business for 14 years, and when it broke up in 1994, I entered a period of serious reflection. I had really enjoyed some of my earlier experience in the financial services industry because it allowed me to examine the family business outside of the standard insurance general agent model. So while I loved helping people build, protect, and preserve their wealth, I was eager to approach this task from a fresh new angle.

Dan Sullivan: Now, you were surveying the industry at a time when critical firewalls were being removed.
Debra Schatzki: Yes. And in 1999, I got lucky: The tax law changed in New York and finally allowed financial services divisions to be

part of an accounting firm. So I set out to find and scrutinize the up-and-coming accounting firms in New York.

Dan Sullivan: How were you evaluating these accounting firms? Is there an ideal size for your type of process?
Debra Schatzki: Small and medium-sized firms with under 30 partners are usually best for financial advisors to work with. But it's really not the number of partners that is important; it's the decision-making and leadership structures within the organization. I'm very comfortable working on the high end in areas like retirement and estate planning, so I wanted to be with a firm that was operating in these areas.

Dan Sullivan: And you found this at Marcum & Kliegman, LLP?
Debra Schatzki: Yes. At the time, Marcum & Kliegman, LLP was, and still is, the fastest growing accounting firm in New York. I hit it off with Jeffrey Weiner, the managing partner, and in a half-hour conversation using The Strategy Circle®*, I was able to demonstrate the possibilities of collaboration. I went back for some more meetings to present my ideas to the other partners, and soon I was introduced to the entire firm as the managing director of their financial services division. In 2007, continuing our affiliation with Marcum & Kliegman, we joined Weiser LLP, where I am president of Weiser Capital Management LLC. Weiser LLP is the ninth largest accounting firm in the New York metro area and one of the top ten fastest growing firms in the country.

Dan Sullivan: What kind of agreement were you operating with, because I'm sure that you brought a lot of new business to the firm on day one?
Debra Schatzki: We agreed that the accounting firm would split the compensation of all the business I brought in, whether from my clients or their clients. In the first year, I brought in 80 percent of the business, and, you know, a lot of people look at that and say, "What, are you crazy? Why would

    *For the definition of The Strategy Circle, please see page 229.

you go into an accounting firm, bring in 80 percent of the business, and actually wind up giving it away?"

Dan Sullivan: How did you respond?
Debra Schatzki: Well, I wasn't giving it away exactly. The firm was picking up substantial overhead and personal expense. And I viewed it as a training period, an adjustment period. What kept me going were the relationships I developed with some very entrepreneurial accountants. For example, the managing partner referred some really exciting clients to me. I also had the opportunity in this early period to meet with all the partners individually and go over the benefit planning, the business planning that the accounting firm actually did. When it became clear to the partners that I wasn't just there to make a sale, but was really trying to develop a long-term model that would be great for the firm, they became much more invested in the process and began to create opportunities.

Dan Sullivan: You know, Debra, I've been dealing with financial advisors for 30 years, and I must have a hundred examples of financial advisors who have tried to make some sort of teamwork with accounting firms work, and it has failed for them. From your perspective of success, what are some of the obstacles and challenges that can undermine these efforts?
Debra Schatzki: Language is the first obstacle, Dan. Being a financial advisor, being a "salesperson," I speak a very different language than accountants. On one level, the challenge is simply semantical. So I've learned to translate all my operations and sales materials into language that accountants can understand. But the broader challenge is one of communication style. When I look at a client, I see all of the opportunities; whereas, accountants are often inclined by necessity to focus on the problems. I don't want to generalize here, but, clearly, different professions approach the same situation from different angles. As a financial advisor in an accounting firm, I can only communicate effectively if I understand the mindset of my colleagues.

Dan Sullivan: As you talk, Debra, it strikes me that this challenge of language and communication is something that all my clients face on a daily basis when they interact with colleagues who haven't been exposed to Strategic Coach terminology and concepts, who can't speak D.O.S.

Debra Schatzki: That's definitely true, Dan. I think in my own case, the key is to be very clear and firm about directing the meetings when they involve my area of expertise.

Dan Sullivan: How do financial advisors build that trust and cooperation with the accountants? I mean, is there a certain attitude or professional background that's best suited to this type of arrangement?

Debra Schatzki: That's an interesting question. I was involved with The Leading Edge, a producer group for accounting firms that includes all of the financial services divisions within those firms. One of the things I noticed at their meetings was that the financial advisors came from very different backgrounds. Some had grown up in the investment community, others the insurance community.

Dan Sullivan: Do they primarily gravitate to those areas of expertise once inside the accounting firm?

Debra Schatzki: Yes, I've found advisors who go to an accounting firm and say, "We're going to start a financial services division," yet they focus almost exclusively on investments or insurance. To a certain extent, this type of specialization is understandable because it allows each advisor to focus on their Unique Ability®. But we always emphasize that for financial services divisions to succeed over the long term, they should be comprehensive and full-service. One of the focuses of my process is to show advisors how they can move beyond their specialty by hiring correctly and really starting to grow a full-functioning division.

Dan Sullivan: Let's talk about that process, then, Financial

Services In A Box (FSIB), which is a "plug-and-play" tool box for developing, implementing, and successfully supporting financial services divisions within an accounting firm.

Debra Schatzki: Accounting firms are like living organisms with distinct professional structures. It's very important to shape the financial services division around these structures in a way that is compatible with the firm's unique dynamics. So the first stage or tool is The Qualification Snapshot™, where we gather background information and analyze whether a firm is qualified to host a financial services division. This assessment takes into account factors such as the size of the firm, the decision-making structure, the presence of any specialty areas, and the general receptiveness among partners toward a financial services division.

> Accounting firms are like living organisms with distinct professional structures. It's very important to shape the financial services division around these structures in a way that is compatible with the firm's unique dynamics.

Once a firm is selected, the next step is The Business Planning Process™. We sit down with the partners and really have a frank discussion about their goals and expectations for a financial services division. Everybody needs to be on the same page. We use The D.O.S. Conversation to guide this discussion. Then, building on this information, we formulate a written business plan that incorporates a realistic assessment of their capabilities and clientele.

Dan Sullivan: Does the business plan include actual production projections?

Debra Schatzki: Yes, we talk numbers. It's important to be clear from the beginning of each year about the profit capabilities of the financial services division. One thing that's crucial is that the number reflects a realistic and safe projection because accounting firms hate surprises. If you tell a law firm you're going to do $1 million in production, and you do $700,000, they're thrilled. But not accounting firms. They would much rather have you meet a lower estimate than fall short of a more ambitious goal. It's just the psychology of the profession.

Dan Sullivan: Once the business plan is written down, how do firms move toward implementation?
Debra Schatzki: Well, in the FSIB process, we identify two main keys for successfully implementing the business plan: the Front Stage key, which is having the right financial advisor, and the Back Stage key, which is having the right back office. So a large part of our work with firms and advisors is providing step-by-step support in these areas.

When you're a financial advisor working in an accounting firm, one of the most important things you can do is maintain a presence with the accountants, constantly reminding them of your role and your contributions. Step 3, The Marketing Game Plan™, is really a way to preserve communication, education, and training within the firm and with its clients.

Dan Sullivan: What sort of initiatives does this include?
Debra Schatzki: We really have developed some creative and productive initiatives. For example, every month at Weiser [Weiser Capital Management LLC], a different financial advisor writes a very simple Idea of the Month that comes out of a problem we solved for clients. We describe what happened, and how an accountant can add further value in this or similar situations. Another initiative is our quarterly round tables run by various branches of the financial services division. We have a

The focus here is to develop, implement, and service a marketing plan that allows advisors to continually make contacts and display their capabilities for accountants and their clients.

> This is one of the beautiful things about working in an accounting firm: They have structures in place like human resource divisions and marketing departments to provide back-office support ... The FSIB process is designed to help advisors really leverage these resources and take advantage of the unique technical services available at accounting firms.

retirement expert; group benefit, insurance, and investment experts; enrolled actuaries; and a benefits team. They each do a quarterly round table, and we also pick one team each quarter to be showcased at all of our different offices in front of the managers and accountants. Finally, a couple of times a year, we'll partner up with different law firms or other professional firms to do public seminars.

Dan Sullivan: And these are all initiatives you facilitate for other advisors in the FSIB program.

Debra Schatzki: Yes. The focus here is to develop, implement, and service a marketing plan that allows advisors to continually make contacts and display their capabilities for accountants and their clients. This is one of the beautiful things about working in an accounting firm: They have structures in place like human resource divisions and marketing departments to provide back-office support. For instance, at Weiser, there's a tax department, audit services, litigation support, a family office, and valuator services. These are just some of the back-office resources a financial professional can make use of at a good accounting firm. The FSIB process is designed to help advisors really leverage these resources and take advantage of the unique technical services available at accounting firms.

Dan Sullivan: This process is phenomenal, Debra, and I know you've had great success implementing it at different accounting firms. At what stage did you realize that you could package this process for other financial advisors?

Debra Schatzki: I was actually on a plane, on the way to my Strategic Coach workshop. That particular session was focused on developing intellectual capital, so I had done some preparation. On the plane, I began to realize that my process really could be packaged because there's a marketplace logic in integrating accounting firms and financial advisors. But even more important, I realized that Financial Services In A Box is simple and easy to understand, even if the challenge of establishing these financial services divisions can be daunting. And with my own personal success with accounting firms, I knew the process had proven credibility that would appeal to advisors.

Dan Sullivan: You also work directly with accounting firms, right?

Debra Schatzki: I do have about 20 accounting firms that want us to set up or help them fix their financial services divisions. So my role is to find advisors and match them with the appropriate accounting firm. We have actually created an interview system that has helped us match up advisors and firms.

Dan Sullivan: Debra, I'm an advisor in Dallas, Texas, a long way from Times Square, and I want to do this. What's the first step?

Debra Schatzki: Well, when somebody contacts us, the first thing we do is conduct telephone interviews to determine whether or not this advisor is ready to proceed. Then we put together a preliminary business plan based on conversations with the advisors and accountants. For this we charge a fee. If they decide to continue, we go right to implementing the process, continuing to meet on a quarterly basis.

Dan Sullivan: Start to finish, how quickly can they expect to be operational.

Debra Schatzki: If things go smoothly and we find the right people, they could be operational within one quarter.

Dan Sullivan: Talk about how these advisors retain a plug-and-play relationship with the FSIB tool box once they've linked up with an accounting firm.
Debra Schatzki: What's so effective about our process is that at Weiser, we have a huge wealth of resources and experience that advisors and accounting firms can plug into. Smaller firms that can't afford the kind of staff available at Weiser can plug into ours, and they have access to all the different financial services reps and staff for Back Stage support.

Dan Sullivan: What kind of compensation arrangement are you operating with in these relationships?
Debra Schatzki: The FSIB process has an initial set-up fee and a percentage charge. Eventually, once the subscriber has developed its own back office, the charge is reduced, and FSIB functions in a coaching and consulting capacity.

Dan Sullivan: So, in other words, as this goes nationwide, it becomes a huge profit center for your home firm.
Debra Schatzki: Absolutely. And what's great is that it keeps the partners excited about my own financial services division and committed to expanding our own capabilities.

Dan Sullivan: From an industry transformation perspective, why is your process such a valuable solution for the accounting industry?
Debra Schatzki: It's a powerful solution for a variety of reasons. First, clients

… accounting firms are always looking to increase revenues, and a properly run financial services division can provide an enormous addition to the bottom line.

don't always pay in a timely fashion, but when you offer greater value and more service, they become better payers. I can't tell you how many times accountants have told me how much easier it is collecting fees from clients because of the work we did on the financial services side. Second, accounting firms are always looking to increase revenues, and a properly run financial services division can provide an enormous addition to the bottom line. Finally, liability is a major concern for accounting firms, and producing detailed financial plans can go a long way toward reducing a firm's exposure.

Dan Sullivan: I suspect, Debra, that even though the time available for your own business has been drastically reduced, your personal production keeps growing because of the increased opportunities.
Debra Schatzki: That's definitely true, Dan. This year I probably worked two months in total on my own business. Yet I did 25 percent more in life production and investment this year than last, and I did more fee business.

Dan Sullivan: And you're not wondering where the business is going to come from two or three years down the road.
Debra Schatzki: That's right. I actually am more excited than ever because we now have 18 professionals in Weiser's New York office, three in the Long Island office, and we're starting up our New Jersey practice. What's incredible to me is that so many of the financial services people who have contacted me can clearly see the possibilities of doing business a new way, despite having been part of an older way of doing business for so long, and they can't wait to get involved. Everyone on my team had record production last year.

Dan Sullivan: Looking ahead five years, Debra, where do you see the scope of FSIB? Can you see a thousand firms across the country doing this?
Debra Schatzki: Yes, I actually can.

> The more we can get talented accountants, financial advisors, lawyers, and other professionals working together in cohesive units, the better we can serve the public. Creating value for the client is ultimately what this is all about.

Dan Sullivan: It's going to transform two industries.

Debra Schatzki: I would go even further, Dan, and say that FSIB has the potential to transform the entire professional services industry. I see FSIB as a great tool for helping financial professionals work with other professional firms because it's so easy to implement and so powerful at bridging the language gap, the communication gap. The more we can get talented accountants, financial advisors, lawyers, and other professionals working together in cohesive units, the better we can serve the public. Creating value for the client is ultimately what this is all about.

For contact details on Financial Services In A Box, please see page 233.

IDEA 6

Making Everything Predictable

"I remember how much I used to have to pay attention to what was going on in the industry ... Now I don't pay any attention to any of these things because none of them affect how I use my Unique Process."

Idea 6

Making Everything Predictable

Building a financial practice into a real business.

The Unique Process Advisors in this book, and hundreds more in Strategic Coach, will all tell you that having a Unique Process makes their businesses and their lives more predictable. Here's how Lee Brower experiences this advantage:

"I remember how much I used to have to pay attention to what was going on in the industry. If a company changed leadership, it affected me. If they changed policies, it changed how I could sell. If new products were introduced, or existing ones changed, it changed my selling approach. Then there were all the changes in compliance from the companies, the brokers, and the industry. Almost anything could change how I did business, and the changes kept becoming more unpredictable. It was hard to keep up with them. Now I don't pay any attention to any of these things because none of them affect how I use my Unique Process. The Empowered Wealth Process develops and expands regardless of industry developments, crises, and changes."

Geared to the clientele, not to companies.
The reason Lee Brower and other Unique Process Advisors can ignore developments and events in the financial services industry is that their Unique Processes are independent and self-evolving. They do not depend on any head office input or output. They are an ultimate expression of entrepreneurial freedom. Unique Processes are not governed by regulatory rules and restrictions. Dan Taylor remembers the day he decided to relinquish his industry licenses:

Unique Process Advisors enjoy a continual predictability in all aspects of their business operation. This predictability enables them to plan and implement continual improvements that lead to greater and more accelerated growth.

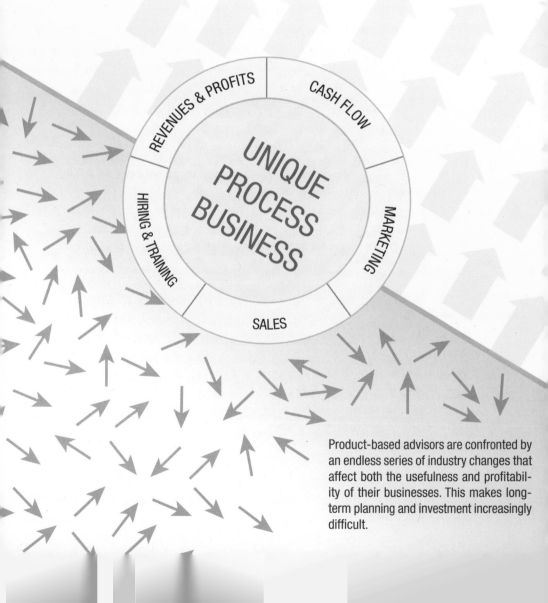

REVENUES & PROFITS

CASH FLOW

HIRING & TRAINING

UNIQUE PROCESS BUSINESS

MARKETING

SALES

Product-based advisors are confronted by an endless series of industry changes that affect both the usefulness and profitability of their businesses. This makes long-term planning and investment increasingly difficult.

"I'd just suffered through a meeting with a twenty-six-year-old compliance lawyer from my broker dealer. She told me that if I didn't submit everything I was doing for her approval, she could see to it that my license was pulled. That seemed like a good idea to me. So I told her that she could have all my licenses because I didn't need them anymore. She was speechless. The next day the broker dealer called to repair the situation, but I told him it was too late. He asked me how I was going to make a living without my licenses. I responded that this was my problem, not his. Over the next month, I moved all of my licensed business to another advisor, who backs me up with all the product sales I need. Since then I've made far more money from my Unique Process than I ever did from selling products."

Dan told us that the moment he no longer had to deal with his broker dealer and with products, his life became much more predictable. The same thing is true of Mary Anne Ehlert:

"When I walked away from my financial company, I was their number one advisor in terms of assets under management out of a sales force of more than ten thousand. But none of this means anything in comparison with the business I'm creating because of The Process For Protected Tomorrows. Before, I always had to deal with the executives' and the compliance peoples' issues. Now I only have to deal with my clients' issues."

All complications and unpredictability come from products.
Since 1974, I have coached more than 6,000 financial advisors from ten countries, representing hundreds of different companies and brokers dealerships. The biggest trend over these three decades for all of these advisors is that business within the industry has become increasingly more complicated and unpredictable, and far less enjoyable. As I analyzed the various issues that advisors have presented to me in Strategic Coach workshops, I identified a single source of most of their troubles and

frustrations: their licensed products. *To the degree that financial advisors depend either wholly or mainly on regulated products for their incomes and security, their lives always get more complicated and less predictable. Or as Scott Keffer puts it:*

"When you have to deal with bureaucrats and regulators, life never gets better; it always gets worse. It never gets simpler; it always gets more complicated and confusing."

Conversely, once these advisors transform their businesses within a Unique Process based on upfront fees for their wisdom and creativity, their lives become increasingly simpler, more predictable, and far more enjoyable. There are five aspects to this greater simplicity and predictability:

1. The Unique Process makes cash flow and profitability more predictable. The clients are charged directly and continually for their participation in the Unique Process. Many of these client relationships will last for decades, with increasing fees being charged for the advisors' growing wisdom and creativity.

2. The Unique Process makes marketing and selling more predictable. Year in and year out, as advisors sell their Unique Process, nothing about its continued development and expansion is governed by bureaucratic or regulatory factors. The Unique Process continually evolves in terms of its value to clients, and marketing and selling it is always focused on them, not regulators and compliance officers.

3. The Unique Process makes product sales more predictable and continually larger. As the Unique Process evolves and becomes more powerful, all product sales associated with it become larger and more predictable.

4. The Unique Process makes hiring and training more predictable. Product-based advisors often have trouble hiring, training, and keeping good staff. The reason for this is the bureaucratic and regulatory complications and aggravations that come with the products. As soon as the main income starts to come from a Unique Process, everything becomes more predictable, more inspirational, and more enjoyable for everyone in the advisor's business.

5. A continually growing business can be built around a Unique Process that is not possible around a product-based practice. Most financial advisors are single salespeople who attempt to do business with one or two staff people at most. Twenty years can pass and their businesses fail to grow because they do not have predictable cash flow and profits. Many of our Unique Process Advisors started out with this "lone wolf" approach. But as soon as they began operating within their Unique Processes, the increased predictability of their businesses and their lives enabled them to begin growing companies to a size that product-based advisors could never dream of. Many Unique Process Advisors have companies with dozens of staff and with revenues of ten or twenty times greater than what they ever achieved when they sold only products.

Tom Miller's VisionLink Solution transforms the ability of business owners to make organizational growth more predictable. In doing so, his Unique Process has made his own business success more predictable. Let's read how he is doing this.

Tom Miller
The VisionLink Solution™

Tom Miller, a long-time client of Strategic Coach, has created a fundamental solution for growing companies in the $10 million to $200 million market, answering the question, "How can companies use their compensation programs to help drive long-range growth?" Tom, a highly successful financial advisor with over 30 years' experience, went from commodity sales to a Unique Process in his own practice. In this transition, he also created an easily transferable model — The VisionLink Solution™ — that dozens of other financial advisors are now using to transform their market differentiation, success, and satisfaction.

Dan Sullivan: Thanks for joining us today, Tom. Why don't you begin by talking a little about your background in the financial services industry, and how The VisionLink Solution came to conception?

Tom Miller: Well, I started in the financial services industry over 30 years ago, and I suppose I had a fairly traditional career, although I didn't do a lot of "kitchen table work," so to speak. My clientele always consisted of small- to mid-sized business owners, and my focus tended to be on solving the basic financial services needs of these owners. But over time I discovered that having a product-based approach to solving their problems wasn't really satisfying, so I started to get into the financial planning arena and did a lot of fee-based planning. Eventually, I began to get interested in the world of executive compensation as an extension of my financial services work with business owners. I discovered when I went into the marketplace that the insurance and financial services industry had a totally different conception of executive compensation than the business owners themselves.

Dan Sullivan: Was that because of the product orientation?

> I discovered when I went into the marketplace that the insurance and financial services industry had a totally different conception of executive compensation than the business owners themselves.

Tom Miller: Exactly. What people in the financial services business were doing, including me, was focusing on one or two areas of the compensation world, particularly those areas that would be satisfied with the delivery of an insurance product. But the other needs of business owners were being neglected.

Dan Sullivan: When did this occur to you?
Tom Miller: Well, I remember the exact client who turned on the light bulb. He was the CFO of a small public company for whom we had done a deferred compensation plan. He asked me, "What other types of executive compensation work do you do?" My response was, "What do you have in mind?" He described some of the issues he was dealing with, and I determined we could probably help him with those. Next thing you know, we were doing all sorts of compensation planning for a fee without relying on insurance products.

Dan Sullivan: In other words, you began moving closer to the consulting end of the business.
Tom Miller: That's right. Large companies rely on "pure compensation consultants" like Hewitt, Mercer, and Watson Wyatt to develop compensation strategies for their employees.

Dan Sullivan: But you really zeroed in on small- to mid-sized private companies.
Tom Miller: Exactly. We're talking about companies in the $10 million to $200 million revenue range, with between 75 and 1,500 employees. If you're a company of this size looking for assistance in the compensation area, the fees of the large firms can be pretty prohibitive. That's what's so valuable about our process. We've developed a way to provide comparable, if

not superior, services at a price point that is much more appropriate for those small- to mid-sized employers.

Dan Sullivan: So how are you able to reach these companies?
Tom Miller: We've discovered that by making these services available in the private marketplace, we receive many referrals from CPAs, attorneys, and other advisors.

Dan Sullivan: I would bet there's also more of an untapped demand for these services among small and mid-sized companies.
Tom Miller: That's a good point, Dan. If I ask a small business owner who has never talked to a compensation consultant how effective compensation programs are on a scale from one to ten, he'll admit they're probably at a two or a three. So we can apply our process and add instant value that he can immediately see.

Dan Sullivan: Let's talk about that process.
Tom Miller: Well, the first stage of The VisionLink Solution is called Vision Definition. And here we're concerned with identifying the two visions within the company—that of the owners and that of the employees—and then using this foundation to generate a broad "compensation philosophy statement" that will lay out the general principles guiding the pay strategies and rewards programs within the company.

Dan Sullivan: How do you identify those visions?
Tom Miller: We spend time speaking with the owner about his plans for the business. We need to get clear on their vision for the future company and how they plan to fulfill it. We discover not only what that vision looks like, but why it's important to them. We also want to quantify the value of the future company. How much new value will be created over the next few years? This will become an important part of the compensation discussion. We'll want to know if the business owner can identify the total, in both direct and indirect compensation.

We'll also want to know how the business measures its return on that investment, or even if it considers that compensation an investment as opposed to an expense. And what we emphasize is that every business owner should envision some type of return on their present company as if they were taking that net equity and investing it in the marketplace. Of course, great companies should improve on the rate of return that the market gives you. And that excess return can only be generated if you have great people helping you achieve it. So the question of compensation really becomes a question of how much of that value you should share with those core, growth-generating employees because, over the long run, you need to have those people satisfied.

Dan Sullivan: Now, you also talk with the employees themselves, right?
Tom Miller: Yes. We ask the employees a series of questions in private. For example, if we were working with your employees, Dan, the first question would be, "Tell me where this company is going, tell me where Dan and Babs are leading this company. What is Strategic Coach going to look like in the future?" Second, we ask them to address how the company is going to reach its goals: What are the key initiatives and strategies that have to be launched or maintained in order to achieve that vision? The third question is a bit more personal: "What are you, as an employee, expected to contribute to that growth?" And, finally, the linchpin question is, "What's in it for you? What kind of financial rewards do you expect for this contribution?" These four questions comprise what we call the "Rewards Pyramid" because the conversations culminate in the very real issue of rewards.

Dan Sullivan: Do the owners get the answers back?
Tom Miller: Yes, but what's interesting is that before we even talk to the employees, we present these questions to the owners and ask them to envision how their employees would respond.

Then we'd say something along the lines of, "How confident are you that you'll be satisfied and excited about these answers?" Ultimately, our goal is to make certain that all of the employees can answer those questions in a way that would make the owner very satisfied.

> I like to say that it's better to design a B+ compensation plan with A+ communication than an A+ plan with B+ communication.

Dan Sullivan: This isn't a hypothetical model, though. You actually do go and interview the employees.
Tom Miller: Yes, and these are incredibly rich conversations. The results give the owners more insight into the attitude of their employees than perhaps anything they've ever done.

Dan Sullivan: What's striking about this model, Tom, is that you've created sort of an internal communications operation for the company.
Tom Miller: Strong, open communication is a critical component of effective compensation management. I like to say that it's better to design a B+ compensation plan with A+ communication than an A+ plan with B+ communication.

Dan Sullivan: Now, what's the next stage?
Tom Miller: The Plan Creation stage is where we build on the foundation of the Vision Definition and compensation philosophy to create a comprehensive, powerful compensation program. And, of course, we perform technical analysis and extensive modeling to be sure the plan will build value for the owner as well as the employees.

Dan Sullivan: I know you have a very distinct system for dividing up compensation components. Could you expand on that?
Tom Miller: Sure. Most private companies operate with what I call a "typical compensation allocation." They pay a salary, they

may have some type of short-term incentive plan, and then they introduce a retirement plan—maybe a 401(k) and at least some basic insurance benefits. In contrast, we employ a process called the Total Rewards Assessment. It includes eight potential types of pay. It looks at the total rewards opportunity through three lenses: one, how well are we addressing our employees' cash flow needs; two, how well are we addressing their security needs; and, three, how well are we addressing their wealth accumulation needs? We teach the owner how successful companies use this approach to win the talent wars and focus their employees on driving great results.

Dan Sullivan: What happens when a plan has been formalized? What sort of strategies do you use in the implementation phase?

Tom Miller: Dan, implementation is the most important part of the entire process. We call it the Vision Alignment stage. The objective is to create "line of sight" within the company. "Line of sight" means that employees see a clear connection between their strong job performance and excellent pay. The focus is to create a clear understanding in the mind of key contributors about the relationship between compensation components and the participant's role in the organization.

> ... it all comes back to communication, and the primary focus throughout the implementation phase is always on using the compensation plan as the vehicle for aligning the visions of employees and employer.

Dan Sullivan: This is where The Rewards Reinforcement Strategy™ comes in, right?

Tom Miller: Yes. The Rewards Reinforcement Strategy is a comprehensive process designed to implement, market, and promote the compensation plan to create that "line of sight." And we have a variety of successful strategies for managing the

Back Stage components of the plan's administration, the legal and regulatory issues, and the ongoing financial elements of the plan. But again, it all comes back to communication, and the primary focus throughout the implementation phase is always on using the compensation plan as the vehicle for aligning the visions of employees and employer. We often find, Dan, that companies will invest more money in the implementation process than in the design of the plan itself.

Dan Sullivan: This process is very impressive, Tom. Why don't you talk a bit about having a Unique Process approach rather than the conventional consulting approach or product approach, because you really have created a "third way" here?
Tom Miller: Clearly, our process is a factor that really differentiates us from anyone who would consider themselves our competitors. The biggest mistake most compensation consultants make is launching a plan and then walking away from it. We explain to the client that there is an ongoing responsibility on both sides to manage the plan. That's why the last stage of our process is called Strategic Review. It incorporates ongoing feedback and the continual assessing and rebalancing of the plan. What our process does is keep both sides honest and focused on the goals at hand. The clients know right from the beginning that our relationship will not be tied to any rainmaker, any single person; it's the process that makes the planning work.

Dan Sullivan: I'm sure you've also found, though, that focusing on the process actually enables you to sell a lot more products.
Tom Miller: Absolutely. I've found that the less you worry about getting to the product, the sooner you get to the product, and the more product you actually deliver to your clients. The product becomes one of the tools in the toolkit that ultimately has to be brought out because it's there to solve a particular need that comes up during the course of implementing some plans.

> ... the actual product sale has become quicker, more efficient, and easier. The client has developed such a great relationship with us that when it's time to actually talk product, their basic attitude is "Just get it done, whatever it takes."

Dan Sullivan: What kind of numbers are we talking about here?

Tom Miller: What's been interesting for us is that consulting fees and ongoing servicing fees now make up about 70 percent of our firm's revenue, and that's a change from approximately 15 percent seven or eight years ago. But our commission revenue has expanded as well, so the net dollar amount in product commission has increased even though the proportion has become much more balanced. And the actual product sale has become quicker, more efficient, and easier. The client has developed such a great relationship with us that when it's time to actually talk product, their basic attitude is, "Just get it done, whatever it takes."

Dan Sullivan: Well, that's not surprising because I'm sure your process is incredibly gratifying for these companies. What are some of the crucial changes and improvements you've seen in companies after they get involved with The VisionLink Solution?

Tom Miller: The main thing, Dan, is what happens in the minds of the shareholders, the owners of the company. They have a fresh outlook on the role of compensation as a growth-generator within the company. They know how much they're investing in compensation each year, and now they have tools to measure the return on that investment.

Dan Sullivan: Now, Tom, your process has had a transformative effect, not only on the businesses of your clients but on the entire world of compensation consulting. Talk about your efforts to train and license other advisors in the use of The VisionLink Solution.

Tom Miller: I had never even thought about going down that road until several years ago when I spoke at an industry meeting. Afterwards I was approached by advisors who came up to me asking how they could participate in this. Eventually, we developed a member firm program where we license our services and train qualified financial advisors in the VisionLink process.

Dan Sullivan: What kind of support services do you provide?
Tom Miller: We've created a prototype Front Stage/Back Stage service offering where we provide, through our technical team, the back-office construction, analysis, and development of the deliverables that are presented to the client. This has enabled us to create a truly national firm with advisors in 25 different cities.

Dan Sullivan: What sort of qualities are you looking for when it comes to signing up new advisors?
Tom Miller: I would say the first condition is that the advisor has some experience in the business marketplace—some experience talking to business owners and CEOs about their business needs or even personal needs. They need to have the confidence to walk into a business owner's office and conduct an effective D.O.S. interview. But probably the most important factor is that the advisor is not overly product-oriented. We've had some people look at this as a scheme or trick to sell products. They'll even say, "You can have all the fees, Tom, if we can have the commission." We're not interested in that type of model.

Dan Sullivan: For those advisors who do have the proper mindset for your process, how long, start to finish, before someone is really doing an effective job?
Tom Miller: I would say the advisors who have had the most success are those who were already pretty close to this kind of service offering, dealing in high-end benefits to the business marketplace. These advisors enter the process with a handful of clients who are ready and eager for this type of compensation

... I'm not feeling like my mission in life is to sell a product to somebody whether they need it or not. My mission now is focused on really improving not only the lives of business owners, but of all the employees that work in those businesses.

planning. And so the advisors are able to get some projects off the ground right away. Still, we tell most advisors that they should look at this partnership with us as a minimum three-year transition. But if they're patient with it, and see it as having a long-term impact on the transformation of their business, they should start generating significant success before the end of the first year.

Dan Sullivan: You know, Tom, this model has such big implications, not only for the compensation consulting world, but for the country itself. I've read many articles on the global economic scene, and they all say that the strength or weakness of any national economy relies purely on the performance of small- to mid-sized companies, the type of companies you're working with.

Tom Miller: That's definitely exciting because as we expand to incorporate more and more advisors, our ability to impact that critical market only increases. Many of our advisors are working in small communities with self-made businessmen, and it's certainly gratifying to have this kind of impact.

Dan Sullivan: What has it done for you, Tom, this complete transformation of your own business?

Tom Miller: The interesting thing, Dan, is that my life has actually become a little more complicated. Instead of just running a local Southern California practice, I have relationships with people all over the country, and I'm managing a larger, more complicated business. But it's certainly well worth it. And the reason is that I'm not feeling like my mission in life is to sell a product to somebody whether they need it or not. My mission now is focused on really improving not only the lives of business owners, but of all the employees that work in those businesses.

Dan Sullivan: And the communities where they're located.
Tom Miller: That's right. Our goal for every business we work with is to create more value for the owners and the employees, and that strengthens individual lives and individual communities. I believe that we have the capacity to become the largest, most transformational compensation consulting firm in the country. I look back at how far we've come, but I know even bigger things are in store. It's taken a lot of work to get to this point, but creatively I'm more stimulated and excited than at any point in my career, and I expect that energy to carry this business far into the future.

For contact details on The VisionLink Solution, please see page 232.

IDEA 7

Attracting Talent And Opportunity

"I'm 20 times more successful and a lot more low-key than when I was selling product. Every year, my overall team gets bigger and better, and the reason is that my Unique Process continually encourages and rewards their continued growth of capability."

Idea 7

Attracting Talent And Opportunity

Bypassing personality power for process power.

I've been coaching financial advisors for over 30 years. During tens of thousands of hours of conversation with them, I've noticed two persistent problems that most commodity-based advisors seldom overcome:

• The inability to create powerful teams around them.

• The inability to develop a marketplace of prospects and clients that continually provides bigger opportunities.

What we have discovered, however, is that having a Unique Process solves both of these problems in systematic, permanent ways. Lee Brower, like the other advisors in this book, spent many years being frustrated by these two obstacles:

"Before I developed the Wealth Empowerment process, I found it very difficult to build a team around me. There was nothing in my training as an insurance agent that told me how to develop an organization that would continually get better. But my process has made this possible. And there was nothing that told me how to develop my marketplace in a way that the opportunities would keep getting bigger and better. The Unique Process has also made this possible. My experience was common to everyone who came up through the agency system. We were trained to be dependent on the support system and marketing efforts of head office organizations. The only way they can escape from this dependency is by having a Unique Process."

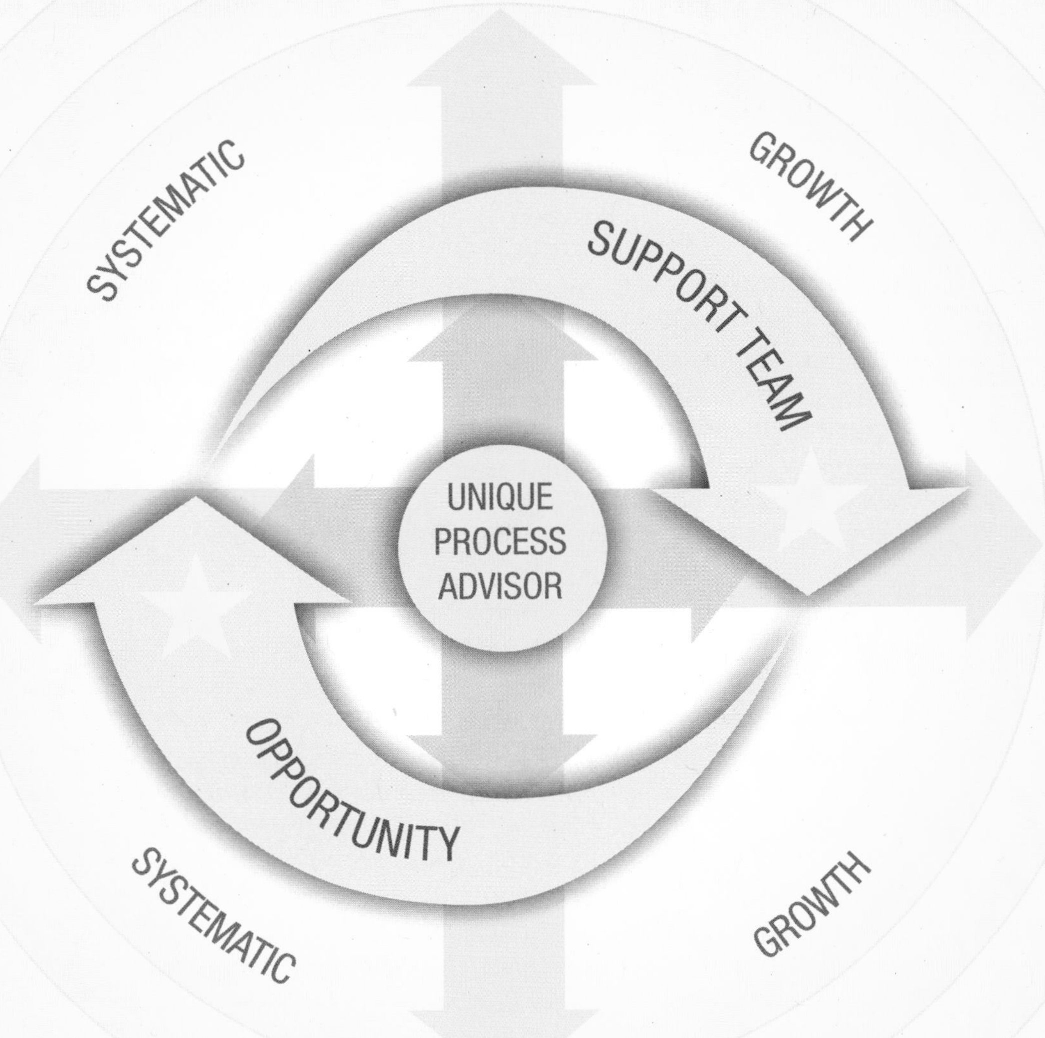
SYSTEMATIC
GROWTH
SUPPORT TEAM
UNIQUE PROCESS ADVISOR
OPPORTUNITY
SYSTEMATIC
GROWTH

Two competitive advantages over commodity-based advisors.
My conversations with over 6,000 financial advisors since 1974 confirms that Lee's experience was, and still is, the rule in the financial services industry. The vast majority of commodity-based advisors don't know how to transform their sales practices into independent, strategic, continually growing entrepreneurial businesses. On the other hand, all of the Unique Process Advisors that we work with in Strategic Coach know how to do this. They continually enjoy two competitive advantages over commodity-based advisors in the marketplace:

- They find that their Unique Process enables them to attract, train, and develop skilled, enthusiastic, and committed teams.

- They find that their process enables them to develop and expand their marketplace opportunities in a strategic fashion that leads to increased revenues and profits— regardless of what is taking place in the economy and the financial industry.

Rob Darnbrough clearly sees both of these advantages at work in his success since he developed his Unique Process:

"I deal with dozens of the top advisors in Canada who are still totally dependent on product sales. The biggest thing I notice about their practices is a continual uncertainty about the future. They find it difficult to plan big because they don't have the support team necessary for bigger results. And they don't know if the bigger, better prospects will be there to provide the commissions necessary to build a team. The way many of them talk about their businesses, you sense that they feel success is a matter of luck. A good year occurs when they have good luck. Bad luck means a bad year. Because they don't have a Unique Process, they don't know how to manufacture 'good luck' every year."

Let's look at each of these advantages more deeply.

- **Attracting, training, and developing a great team:** One of the ironies of being a commodity-based advisor is that success largely comes not from the product, but through "personality power." By this I mean that, over time, successful commodity advisors have to depend more and more on their individual personalities to attract and keep staff members. They are like professional magicians in that the members of their support staff don't really know how the sales occur, or how the money that pays their salaries is actually earned. The support team of a commodity-based advisor is largely ignorant of where future money is going to come from. Everything depends upon their "magical" advisor, and the staff members generally become dependent, passive, and reactive. When the advisor is not there, nothing new or creative can occur.

- **Process power:** Unique Process Advisors, on the other hand, attract their staff through the growing power of their process. They keep their team enthusiastic and committed by showing them how the process solves fundamental problems and creates increasing revenues in the marketplace. Every team member knows how and why the money is earned, and how and why more of it will be earned in the future. Each of them has a personal stake and plays a crucial role in the growth of the company. Unique Process Advisors develop their teams by giving them greater responsibility and authority over a growing number of the stages of the Unique Process.

Debra Schatzki contrasts her transition from relying on personality power to utilizing process power:

"Anyone who knows me knows I have a strong personality, and I knew how to use it to sell product. But after a while, you realize that your business can never get any bigger than your personality. Now that I have Financial Services In A Box, I find that I don't have to be on stage all the time. I'm 20 times more

successful and a lot more low-key than when I was selling product. Every year, my overall team gets bigger and better, and the reason is that my Unique Process continually encourages and rewards their continued growth of capability."

Developing a bigger marketplace in a strategic fashion.
Because their whole team is knowledgeably and creatively involved at every stage, Unique Process Advisors are able to develop and expand market opportunities in a strategic fashion. Over time, the advisors themselves are focused only on those stages of the process where they have a Unique Ability®. Their process is easy to refer, and they have dozens of satisfied clients selling for them every day. New clients realize from the start that there is a whole team involved, not just a single "magical" personality. When the advisor is not there, solutions are still being created by the team members, who continually become more skillful, confident, and responsible. When the advisor is not working, new opportunities are being captured and new money is being made. Lee Brower told us about his own jump in confidence when he realized that he had a true business:

"For the first time, my Unique Process gave me a sense that this was a substantial company, one that my best business clients took as seriously as they did their own. They didn't look at me as an insurance peddlar, but as a professional colleague."

When Charlie Epstein began to focus on the retirement income market about nine years ago, he quickly became frustrated. There was no place to get the training and education he needed to work in this complex area of financial planning. His frustration led to the creation of his Unique Process, The 401k Coach Program, which is attracting talented financial advisors who desire the training and expertise that Charlie's process can offer them. Let's look more closely at how Charlie started on this path and at his transformational Unique Process.

Charlie Epstein
The 401k Coach® Program

Charlie Epstein, a long-time participant in the Strategic Coach Program, has brought great clarity, simplicity, and productivity to a very complex and disorganized industry. Not only has he created a highly profitable 401(k) Unique Process within his own business, he has created a national "school" based on that process that is enabling thousands of financial advisors to transform their whole approach to marketing and implementing 401(k) plans. What is interesting in Charlie's report on his progress is how many different kinds of "clients" have benefited from his creativity: employees, employers, financial advisors, broker dealers, and the financial corporations themselves.

Dan Sullivan: Before we start discussing your process, Charlie, can you give us some background on your early career in the financial services industry and how The 401k Coach® Program came to fruition?

Charlie Epstein: Well, Dan, I came out of college with an economics degree and an interest in theater. I like to tell people that I really had two options: I could either go down to New York City and become a starving actor with my friends; or I could move back to Springfield, Massachusetts, get into the life insurance business, and have no friends. So, of course, I chose the second option, and I got started selling life insurance as a company agent in 1979. Then in 1983, I decided to create Epstein Financial Services to differentiate myself a little bit from the industry—working for the client rather than a particular insurance company.

Dan Sullivan: But you were still product based.

Charlie Epstein: Yes. For a good period of time, I was very successful—agent of the year, Lives Leader, everything that you

> My wall was covered with plaques and awards, but my life was cluttered, running from sale to sale. I really didn't know who I was to the end user, the people I was selling all of these products to.

could hope for at that particular time in the industry. My wall was covered with plaques and awards, but my life was cluttered, running from sale to sale. I really didn't know who I was to the end user, the people I was selling all of these products to. I had reached The Ceiling of Complexity*. So in 1990, I decided to join the Strategic Coach Program. And thank goodness, because without that decision, I'd still be a life insurance agent getting all those awards but without a clue how to create real value.

Dan Sullivan: Once a person comes to the realization that creating value is what they should be focusing their efforts on, it changes how they think about their business. Was that your experience, Charlie?

Charlie Epstein: Yes it was. This was the point when I really began to transform my business. Specifically, I was approached by a large accounting firm in town, and they wanted to partner up with somebody who could provide something different to their clients. Out of this conversation, I created our first Unique Process, which we called The Family CFO®. The premise was really simple: Every company has a CFO; we wanted to be your family CFO. It was a shift to the fee business, and we were very successful. But I knew something was missing. I knew I could create even more value, and have an impact on the wider society. I started focusing on the 401(k) market as a place to leverage my capabilities and my relationship with the accounting firm.

Dan Sullivan: How long ago was this?

Charlie Epstein: About six years ago. But it was frustrating trying to get into the 401(k) business because there was no "university" of retirement planning. There was no place to get the training and education that I needed. This was a very pressing issue for me because we had decided to create a third-party administrative firm to administer and design retirement plans as part of our 401k Coach® Retirement Plan Solution™.

Dan Sullivan: How did you intend to sell the plans?
Charlie Epstein: That was the question, Dan. We could hire an outside wholesaler to sell our services. But those people are expensive. So I began to think, hey, wouldn't it be good to actually train our own advisors on how to build a retirement plan business? We took 20 advisors, life insurance agents who had never sold a retirement plan, and trained them through a Unique Process I developed called The 401k Coach Retirement Plan Solution. Within two years, these advisors made our third-party administrative firm the number one third-party administrator in America for a major institution.

Dan Sullivan: Wow.
Charlie Epstein: That's what I said. "Wow! I think we're on to something here." So that was the genesis of The 401k Coach Program. All the money they paid us, we plowed back into R&D and our marketing material, and we went down to the American Society of Pension Actuaries 401(k) Sales Summit in the beginning of 2003 and had our coming-out party. Now, over 500 advisors have participated in our program. We're looking to expand our membership to 1,000 in the next three years.

Dan Sullivan: That's just outstanding, Charlie. Now, why don't you detail the different stages of your process? How do you actually go about training these advisors?
Charlie Epstein: Well, this is an extraordinarily complex business. There's so much information involved. So it's critical when you're training advisors to cover all the bases. We've developed a three-year program, and advisors sign up a year at a time. Whether they're veterans or newbies to the retirement

plan industry, in the first year, we help our members address the Ten Critical Components to Building a Retirement Plan Business. So the first critical component is what we call the Pre-Call Research System™. Do you have a repeatable system of success in your practice that you use to garner the greatest amount of information about a 401(k) plan or business that you're about to call on? In other words, when you walk into that first meeting, are you armed with more information and knowledge than the plan sponsor or sponsors that you're about to meet with?

Dan Sullivan: What about after that?
Charlie Epstein: Critical component number two is what we call The Five Levels of Client Creation™. To be successful at generating new prospects, you've got to be firing on all five levels of client creation. This system produces qualified referrals, not just any referrals. These referrals come from superior centers of influence that help you in getting to those qualified prospects on your "wish list" of people you want to do business with. The third component is The 401(k) Business Development Matrix™. I'm absolutely amazed as I go around the country and speak with entrepreneurs in this business who, as a majority, don't know their profit margin. They don't know how to price their business. You have to understand how the product is built, how the institution is pricing it, and, most important, you need to know one very important number and that's your margin.

Critical component number four is what we call The 401k Coach Retirement Plan Solution. You have to create a process or a solution that differentiates your practice in the marketplace, sets you apart from your competitors, and, in the process of doing that, reduces your expenses. The 401k Coach Retirement Plan Solution is a turnkey evolutionary sales and marketing system that communicates the Front Stage steps of our process to clients, and outlines the Back Stage processes we use to fulfill those steps. Critical component number five is the technical side of our business: "To Be Or Not To Be A Fiduciary"™. The first question we ask in this component is, "Do you understand what it is to be a fiduciary?" In other words, what does it take for a plan sponsor to be a fiduciary? What are the roles and responsibilities that a plan sponsor has? And, how do you as an advisor to that plan assist that fiduciary to meet their fiduciary objectives, standards, goals, and criteria?

Critical component number six is Plan Design and Administration Issues™. As a practitioner, you need to have at least some knowledge in the area of plan design and administrative issues. Critical component number seven is Investment Monitoring and Platform Services™. What is the repeatable system of success you have in place, so that when you meet with a plan sponsor on a quarterly, semi-annual, or annual basis, you have the ability to assist that plan sponsor in meeting their fiduciary obligations by monitoring the investments and understanding the ins and outs of the plan platform?

Dan Sullivan: This covers a lot of ground. What are the final steps?
Charlie Epstein: Number eight is what I call Compelling Selling™. In this component, the plan sponsor becomes part of your repeatable system of success for generating a never-ending stream of qualified referrals from superior centers of influence that, on a regular basis, provides you with introductions to other like-minded business owners because they're thrilled with what you do for them. Critical component number nine is something we call The M2 Effect: The Maggie Factor™. This really looks at building an ongoing relationship with each and every participant in the retirement plan so that you or your team are their first thought, their first choice, and the focal point in the connection between their retirement plan and planning for all of their future financial needs. So, who is Maggie? Maggie is an individual or individuals

that you hire to be your SWAT team. Their only job is to show up every day at your 401(k) plan businesses and meet with the participants of those plans to educate them on everything they need to know to create the greatest opportunities for themselves.

Critical component number ten is what we call The Quantum Leap™. Getting your team to buy into your vision is crucial to your success. The Quantum Leap is about how you manage your practice. By effectively managing your practice, you're acknowledging and communicating with your team in a way that says, "We're constantly working on getting better."

Dan Sullivan: What is the typical profile of the advisors who are attracted to this process?
Charlie Epstein: I like to categorize people along three lines. First, there are the "rookie advisors," with one to three years of experience in the financial services business. They might be attached to a brokerage operation or operating as an investment advisor. When they come in to The 401k Coach Program, we give them a total turnkey process that gets them right into the marketplace. Second, we have the "mid-life crisis" producers who have been in the business for 10 to 15 years. They're hitting The Ceiling of Complexity™, running from product sale to product sale, so they're attracted to the 401(k) business because it allows them to use all the skills they've acquired over the years, while focusing on one niche of the marketplace. Third, we have what I call the "Grizzly Adams" of the industry, guys like me who have been around for 20 to 25 years. They know it all. They've done it all. They've seen it all. But they don't have the time and tenacity to train their associates and employees in the 401(k) marketplace. So what I tell these people is, "You send us a person in your firm, and we'll train them in the Ten Critical Components and our 401k Coach Retirement Plan Solution, so you will have a trained advisor who has the confidence to create value in the 401(k) arena."

Finally, I want to make it clear that we have a large number of experienced advisors in the 401(k) marketplace who want to take their business to the next level and have found our program to be very beneficial to them as well.

Dan Sullivan: It must be valuable for the advisors to interact with colleagues at so many different stages of development.
Charlie Epstein: It's very interesting to watch 35 advisors at different levels in the room, working on their process. We do create a lot of cross-pollination. We've seen older advisors enter partnerships with younger advisors they met in the program. We really do cater to advisors with various levels of experience in the business.

Dan Sullivan: What are the major D.O.S. issues these advisors face?
Charlie Epstein: Well, the advisors really have a number of dangers. Number one, there's the complexity of the 401(k) business and the compliance issues. Our program ensures that the advisor has a process in place that meets the requirements of the law and will assist them in any audits from the Department of Labor. Now the advisor can walk up to the plan sponsor and say, "I will create a fiduciary shield around you as the plan sponsor and me as the advisor. We're going to take care of your employees." The second danger is The Commoditization Trap™. So immediately, in the first session, we ask the advisors to assess their position in the marketplace. The question is, "How am I going to differentiate myself?" We take the advisors through a six-step process called The 401k Coach Retirement Plan Solution, designed to break them out of The Commoditization Trap. Gradually, the advisors begin to separate themselves from the product sales by learning how to demonstrate, on a Front Stage basis, how they can create value for the plan sponsor, the participants, and other parties involved in retirement planning. We call that The Price of Coffee Value Assessor™. It's that epiphany moment when advisors discover how to charge for that "true value."

Dan Sullivan: What about the institutions, the 401(k) platform providers? I know they have a lot of dangers.

Charlie Epstein: The institutions also face a Commoditization Trap. You know, these days all the 401(k) platform providers look the same. It's like Tom Friedman says: "The world is flat." And this is particularly true when it comes to the 401(k) platform; they have the "look-alike syndrome." So we're actually in dialogue with a handful of major institutions about how they can differentiate themselves to the advisor and move beyond that "look-alike" phenomenon in the industry. Three or four years ago, these organizations weren't even calling us. But now we have an institution creating scholarship money for their agents to attend our program. We have institutions that have allocated resources toward training and education for brokers, RIAs, and advisors to attend our programs. We also have multiple institutions that want us to train their wholesalers in the industry. And, one of the fastest growing broker dealers wants to get into the 401(k) marketplace with their advisors and is looking at how our process can help protect them from the litigious society we live in. So, certainly, these are all exciting opportunities that weren't available three or four years ago.

Dan Sullivan: Charlie, let's just give some real practical advice here. What's the turnaround for someone who's reading this interview and interested in The 401k Coach Program?

Charlie Epstein: As soon as someone signs up, we've got programs in place every quarter. Right now, we hold most of them in Hartford, Connecticut, but we'll be starting the first 401k Coach Program on the West Coast in California soon. And then we do have six programs around the country that are going to be sponsored by major institutions. So if people call, they can find out how to get involved in those scholarship programs. But as soon as you sign up, you're in a program within 60 to 90 days.

Dan Sullivan: What kind of results have you seen from the advisors in the program?

Charlie Epstein: The University of Massachusetts at Amherst College of Business surveyed 200 of our advisors who have attended at least one year of The 401k Coach Program and found that they had added $350 million of new assets under management after the first year of the program. On average, an advisor could be adding $20 million to $30 million to their new asset business in the first year of the program.

Dan Sullivan: Well what you're providing for them, Charlie, is a plug-and-play capability. Could you talk more about that?

Charlie Epstein: Sure. I cannot emphasize enough that no matter which retirement platform an advisor may be working with, it plugs right into our process. This also applies to RIAs and registered representatives of broker dealers. They learn what aspects of their Back Stage will plug into the Front Stage of our process. We also have marketing tools they can use, and a diagnostic system for them to work with their team members. And one thing I should add is that right now, people who register for the program can bring their staff for a minimal fee.

Dan Sullivan: One group we haven't talked about, Charlie, is the employees who are ultimately using the 401(k) plans for their retirement security. As I'm sure you know, we have some very large corporations, the bedrock of the American economy, basically neglecting or defaulting on their pension programs. So your process is really coming on the scene at an important time nationally.

> On average, an advisor could be adding $20 million to $30 million to their new asset business in the first year of the program.

Charlie Epstein: Great point, Dan. I've had some opportunities to go and speak to employees about the importance of creating Paychecks for Life. And that's really what this entire 401(k) business is about. You know, we produce a 401k Coach T-shirt. And whenever I travel and wear the T-shirt, people come up and say, "I could really use a 401(k) coach." Or, I get on the airplane, and the flight attendants corner me and say, "Could you help me with my 401(k)?" In fact, one of our program participants landed two clients in one week just by wearing the shirt. It's clear the public is hungry for a solution to this issue.

Dan Sullivan: Of course, it's not only companies reneging on retirement promises, but the government as well, with all the questions about the future of social security. Events may unfold over the next few years where the choice is just taken away from people, and we're going to have to go the privatization route. And basically, what you're saying is, let's do it in a really great way.

Charlie Epstein: Let's do it in a creative way. Let's do it in an entertaining, informative, and educational way. That's The Edu-Tainment Experience™ stage of our process. The system is already in place to solve the problem in the private marketplace—just free the advisor's hand. That's my message to the government. And we think The 401k Coach Program is in a great position to help advisors understand this climate and capture this opportunity.

Dan Sullivan: What has The 401k Coach meant for your own career, Charlie?

Charlie Epstein: It really has been an amazing evolution. What it has done for me, Dan, is freed me up to have a much bigger constituency. I've gone from selling a product to individuals, to selling a process to advisors, the plan sponsor, employees of retirement plans, and the institutions that manufacture products—to being involved with the direction of the entire 401(k) industry. And that's a much bigger conversation, a national conversation.

Dan Sullivan: Looking ahead, Charlie, ten years down the road,

what do you see as the impact of The 401k Coach Program?
Charlie Epstein: Dan, if we have a thousand advisors in our program, and those thousand advisors are dealing with anywhere from 100,000 to 300,000 businesses, that means we're going to be impacting hundreds of millions of employees, teaching them how to create greater successful retirement outcomes. If we get this right, 30 to 40 years from now we will prevent another "government bail-out" of retirees who haven't saved enough money.

Dan Sullivan: That's transformational, Charlie. It sure beats selling product individual by individual.
Charlie Epstein: You know, I think back to when I first started in the life insurance business, when the goal was to get 100 to 200 clients who had a lot of money to take care of. I realized I could either work with 100 to 150 people, or I could touch millions. And we're going to touch millions. So it's exciting to be part of the solution to this national question. When I'm talking to employees who are in their twenties or thirties, I like to jokingly tell them, "When you see me in a wheelchair in my eighties, just walk up and say, 'Hey old man, thanks a lot. I'm retired at fifty-five.'" So it's that kind of inspiration that makes me think we're going to impact a lot of lives, and maybe I'll live beyond eighty-five because of it.

For contact details on The 401k Coach Program, please see page 232.

> I've gone from selling a product to individuals, to selling a process to advisors, the plan sponsor, employees of retirement plans, and the institutions that manufacture products — to being involved with the direction of the entire 401(k) industry.

IDEA 8

Competitors
Become
Customers

"Now the money I make by teaching other advisors my Unique Process is far, far greater than what I make from working with my own clients. It's been a remarkable breakthrough, and we've only started."

Competitors Become Customers

No more fighting over scarce opportunities.

Doug Andrew says that there were two big surprises that came from creating his Unique Process:

"Obviously I was surprised and gratified by how it increased my income dramatically, while liberating me from having to sell products. It was amazing to see how much easier it was to work with my clients, and to see how much more they appreciated what I did for them. But an even bigger discovery was to see how other financial advisors came knocking to ask if I would teach them to do what I was doing. When it first started happening, I wasn't sure I wanted to do that. Did I really want to arm my competitors? That's how you think when you've been trained to sell commodities. Other advisors are competitors. But I quickly changed my mind. Now the money I make by teaching other advisors my Unique Process is far, far greater than what I make from working with my own clients. It's been a remarkable breakthrough, and we've only started."

Doug's second surprise echoes what many other Unique Process Advisors have discovered: *When they start succeeding with their Unique Process, many of their competitors in the marketplace want to become customers.* The unique solutions and advantages they have created for themselves are also very useful to other advisors, who will pay to learn how to use the Unique Process with their own clientele. There are several reasons for this:

C

1. The process of commoditization increases every year. The number of different kinds of financial products being sold by thousands of different companies is incalculable. Financial consumers can't tell one product or company from another. This makes it impossible for financial advisors to differentiate themselves on the basis of the products they sell, or the companies they represent. On top of this, regulatory restrictions continually make it even more difficult for product-based advisors to communicate why and how they are better than their competitors. *Unique Process Advisors offer a creative, permanent way to escape from this Commoditization Trap.*

2. Companies cannot provide custom-designed solutions. The financial corporations that manufacture financial products are only good at designing and marketing commodities. They do this solely in order to increase their assets under management. They have no other reason or way to be in business. Therefore, there is no talent, incentive, or means at head offices to provide financial advisors with custom-designed marketing solutions that will make the advisors less dependent on commoditized products. *Unique Process Advisors, on the other hand, are uniquely skillful at creating transformative solutions in the marketplace that other advisors can easily and quickly custom-design for themselves.*

3. Advisors respect the wisdom of innovative advisors. Financial advisors are like soldiers with combat experience. They respect the battlefield wisdom of their experienced comrades-in-arms much more than they do the general knowledge of officers back at headquarters. Executives and managers in financial bureaucracies have little or no practical experience in dealing firsthand with individual clients and their specific issues. *Unique Process Advisors, on the other hand, are "battle-tested" innovators who provide an exciting plan and path for higher income, dramatically less commoditization, and greater entrepreneurial freedom.*

Charlie Epstein, with his 401k Coach Program, provides hundreds of advisors with a platform that makes it possible to differentiate themselves in a completely commoditized industry. In doing so, he is providing a solution for many other parties:

"The 401(k) marketplace is much more complicated than selling life insurance or selling investments. Everyone—the government, politicians, financial companies, regulators, broker dealers, employers, and frequently unions—has their nose in your business. The product, on the face of it, is so commonplace and universally available that it's impossible for advisors to use it to set themselves apart from competitors. But with our approach, it's never about the product. It's about every employee in America having a paycheck for life. And for each employee, there are different issues to consider. The product-based approach can't deal with this. In our process, the advisor becomes the best financial friend that employees ever have. And this solves a big problem for everyone else who is involved in the whole retirement issue."

Weaning themselves off the commodity.

Unique Process Advisors like Doug Andrew and Charlie Epstein are now offering industry-wide solutions in the marketplace that are impossible for financial bureaucracies to create. By using a Unique Process like the ones that Doug and Charlie have created, product-based advisors learn how to wean themselves off their commodity dependency as the sole basis of a client relationship. In this transition, many of them also develop an understanding of how they can create their own Unique Process. Obviously, not every advisor is going to create a Unique Process that will become as significant in the marketplace as the ones featured in this book. Individual advisors differ in terms of creativity, packaging ability, and ambition. But it is possible for tens of thousands more advisors to transform their futures either by licensing a Unique Process from someone else or by developing their own.

Betty Norman, perhaps because of her temperament and counseling background, is sympathetic and appreciative regarding the financial companies:

"I know that there are advisors who complain about the people in head office, but I've been fortunate in the executives and managers I've known. In many ways, they are being commoditized just as much as the advisors. They're dealing with difficult challenges. The company people I work with really would like to be as useful and supportive as possible. I think I've been lucky in having a great deal of enthusiasm from head offices. They've gone out of their way to recommend my Unique Process to their advisors. I think they recognize that I can provide something very valuable that they can't—something that will benefit everyone."

Tens of thousands of Unique Processes.
We started developing the concept and methodology of Unique Process in the mid-1990s. Over that time, I've seen a trend that is now being powered and accelerated by several hundred Unique Process Advisors who are participants in Strategic Coach: The most powerful innovations in value creation are now being developed and disseminated by advisors in the field, rather than by personnel at head office. My sense is that the most important development and transformation of financial advisor skills in the 21st century will take place within these proliferating Unique Processes. I believe that the hundreds of Unique Processes that already exist will evolve and multiply into tens of thousands in the decades ahead.

Doug Andrew used to be focused on selling as much product as possible, in competition with every other advisor. He created his Unique Process to get out of what he saw as an annual rat race. But as soon as the process began to transform his own business, he took it further. In the following interview with Doug, learn how thousands of other advisors are benefiting from his creativity.

Doug Andrew
The True Wealth Transformer™

Many of our Unique Process Advisors have consistently focused on a specific clientele, within a specific market. Over a period of time, they are able to continually deepen their value creation offering. Doug Andrew started off on this path with his Unique Process, The True Wealth Transformer™, focusing on helping his own clientele maximize their wealth creation opportunities. It wasn't long, however, before many other advisors began asking Doug to teach them how to transform their practices in the same dramatic fashion as he had his own. And it was not too long after he began helping thousands of financial advisors to transform their practices that representatives from other financial services sectors made the same request. It's a great story. I think you'll find it instructive and inspiring.

Dan Sullivan: Why don't you begin, Doug, by giving us a little background on your history in the financial services industry?
Doug Andrew: Well, most advisors, as you know, start out selling a commodity, and in 1974, I obtained my insurance license and investment securities license. I began to build a really expansive network doing a lot of personal business with clients, but every ounce of my income was ultimately derived from the sale of a life insurance policy or the setting up of a mutual fund account. But because of the relationship factor, clients were drawn toward my firm's business, and I began to realize that it's not what you're selling but how you make the clients feel that's important. There needs to be a sense of trust and confidence in that relationship.

Dan Sullivan: So you realized pretty early on that you could become commoditized if you didn't capitalize on the unique relationship you'd developed with your clients. What you were doing

> ... I began to realize that it's not what you're selling but how you make the clients feel that's important. There needs to be a sense of trust and confidence in that relationship.

was beginning to align your business around a value creation model.

Doug Andrew: That's right, Dan. I could see that the world indeed loves usefulness, and that I had the ability to establish the type of relationships with my clients that, really, went far beyond the products they were buying from me. I realized that what they really valued was that I was able to provide them with the financial clarity and confidence that they wanted and needed—and were more than willing to pay for. In other words, my clients valued what I brought to our relationship more than even what they got from their accountants or attorneys, for example, because I took the time to be interested in them. So I began to see the value of formalizing this process that I had developed over the years, and packaging and transferring it to other advisors.

Dan Sullivan: Can you talk a bit about how you did that, Doug?
Doug Andrew: First, I upgraded my products from commodities to products that were really unique and differentiating in the industry. And from there, we focused on delivering exceptional service. Pretty soon I had a system in place to rapidly convert people from suspects to prospects to clients. I had developed, in other words, my own system of predictability. I knew that if I put this much wood into the fire in the form of advertising, promotion, and mailers, I would get this much warmth and heat back 90 days later. I knew I could fill up a seminar room with 40 to 60 people and, based on my marketing and prospecting, I could end up with a quarter of a million dollars of revenue 90 days down the road.

Dan Sullivan: And you began to develop a really powerful Unique Process that has deeply impacted clients and now other advisors. Before we go further, could you just detail the various stages of this process?

Doug Andrew: Sure. The process I've used with my clients is called The True Wealth Transformer. It begins with The Enlightenment Experience™, which simply involves attending a seminar, or reading my book and listening to an audio CD. Within 30 minutes of a three-hour seminar, we've transformed the audience's thinking, and they open up to what I'm saying. They go from "I'm listening" to "I'm willing to be influenced" to "I'm signing up for a consultation." At the end of the seminar, I pass out a letter-size sheet of paper with the rest of my Unique Process on it, and I can watch the body language—with husbands and wives nudging each other and saying, "I want that. I want to go through with that process." I'm a strong believer in Dr. Edward Demming's concept that 85 percent of the result is determined in the first 15 percent of any process. So these initial "epiphany moments" are very important. Immediately, they move us away from the commodity level and get people excited.

Dan Sullivan: From a strong opening step, how do you follow that up, Doug?

Doug Andrew: The next step is The True Wealth Discovery™, which is a fact-finding interview where we discover the client's true wealth from their human assets, intellectual assets, financial assets, and civic assets—the four quadrants that Lee Brower teaches in his Empowered Wealth System™. [Editor's note: Lee Brower is a long-time Strategic Coach client and a Unique Process Advisor featured earlier in this book.] And then we move clients into the third step, The Strategic Design™, where we collect all the relevant data and create a 60-page document that shows clients what will happen to them if they keep doing what they're doing—the darkness of night, so to speak. And then we show them the brightness of their future, a future that can be achieved by repositioning assets without increasing outlay by one dime. This step is The Success Formula™.

Dan Sullivan: I'll bet that's a powerful experience for the client. How do you wrap it up?

Doug Andrew: Next we move to The Refinement Stage™ where we do some tweaking and formalizing. Then we present and discuss The Final Action Blueprint™—the plan that the clients will implement. Step seven proceeds with The Implementation Experience™, which involves the actual repositioning of assets and getting the entire plan in place. This step usually takes around four to six weeks. After the plan has been implemented, the final step is called The Accountability Factor™, which involves an annual review to assess and discuss the value we've created for the client.

Dan Sullivan: That's great. Now, Doug, I know that you take a contrarian view in your relationship with your clients. I think that's important to have right out on the table here, because in some circles, it's very controversial. Could you talk a little more about your philosophy on asset repositioning, because it seems to hold an important place in your process?

> Houses were made to house families, not store cash ... I've been teaching people how to leverage and transfer that—how to manage the equity in their property.

Doug Andrew: Well, one of the best examples is all the lazy idle capital that people have in their home. Houses were made to house families, not store cash. One of the strategies I emphasize in my book is how to separate equity from your home and reposition it into investments that are more liquid, safer, and earn a higher rate of return. I mean, during Hurricane Katrina, would you rather have had equity trapped in your house when the levy broke, or in an insurance policy where you could make a phone call and get 50 grand out of it?

There are other products like life insurance, for example, that if it's maximum funded, was designed to store cash. So what's counterintuitive is that I tell people not to go down the highway with one foot on the gas pedal and the other foot on the brake, which is what most Americans do because they accumulate their money in either their house or in their retirement account. They're getting tax breaks on the front end, but they're killing their best partner, Uncle Sam, in the process by paying off their mortgage.

Dan Sullivan: Doug, when was it that you saw the possibility of developing a strategy with your clients?

Doug Andrew: I began to realize back in the mid-1980s that I had helped many, many clients understand that the best way to optimize their assets was to use three "miracles": the miracle of compound interest, the miracle of tax-free accumulation, and the miracle of safe positive leverage. Now, as I said, most Americans accumulate a lot of money in their own home. I've been teaching people how to leverage and transfer that—how to manage the equity in their property.

Dan Sullivan: And then you saw that as being a controlled strategy for your entire financial business approach—basically, the clean-ups of people's actual assets.

Doug Andrew: That's correct, Dan. Not only home equity, but understanding how to better manage the money they're saving for retirement, their IRA and their 401(k). A lot of people, when they hit retirement, wonder whose retirement they were planning—theirs or Uncle Sam's. I've helped numerous clients offset taxes when they begin to withdraw money from their IRA or 401(k) using strategies that are part of my process.

Dan Sullivan: Let's discuss one of the most exciting aspects of your process—the relationships you've developed with other advisors. How did it occur to you that this process has great transferability potential?

> I remember coming home and telling my staff that I was planning to teach this process and charge $3,500 … And they just looked at me like I was crazy. This year our revenue will be ten times what it was three years ago from teaching advisors our Unique Process, and that's just the beginning …

Doug Andrew: People were always coming up to me and saying, "Why don't you teach this, why don't you transfer it?" And I tried some early strategies without much success. It got to the point where I was considering giving up. But during one Strategic Coach workshop in Chicago, Lee Brower was really on my case saying, "Doug, you need to figure out a way to sell your recipe." And you were telling us that you can actually make your competitors your customers. I'll never forget the plane ride home where it really struck me that I could do this. I could package this and charge for it. If I build it, people will come, as the saying goes. I remember coming home and telling my staff that I was planning to teach this process and charge $3,500, and that other advisors would use my book to educate their customers. And they just looked at me like I was crazy. I started my TEAM network of financial services professionals and advisors about five years ago, and now we have more than 2,200 trained TEAM members. Since we began teaching our Unique Process to other advisors, our company revenue has increased tenfold. More important, the average TEAM member realizes a 247 percent increase in their personal income the first year after attending TEAM training. When they return for a refresher session, the average increase in income blossoms to four times what they were earning prior to learning our system.

Dan Sullivan: That's extraordinary, Doug. It's a whole other viable source of income totally apart from selling product.
Doug Andrew: Most definitely. I mean, as we learn in the Coach, when you're out there adding value, new life erupts around you, and it brings you by-products—new surprises, opportunities,

and innovations. I have opportunities I couldn't even envision before starting my Unique Process, and I'm extremely grateful for what I've learned in Strategic Coach to get me here.

Dan Sullivan: Thanks, Doug. Now, from your experience, what sorts of advisors are most interested in entering your program?
Doug Andrew: Well, when I started in Coach2 and became an Intellectual Capital Company, our primary distribution channel was the insurance industry. But I realized that in every seminar, I was generating serious volume for the mortgage industry.

Dan Sullivan: That goes back to the repositioning of assets, right?
Doug Andrew: Yes. I have a strong basis for relationships with mortgage planners. I began to realize that we are an Intellectual Capital Company, first and foremost, with multiple distribution channels in the insurance industry, the mortgage industry, accounting industry, legal industry, real estate industry—all of these people are now coming through my training seminars. I'm bringing people from all different industries together. One of my TEAM members calls this phenomenon "fiscal fusion." And the whole really is greater than the sum of the parts. It's amazing to see how value is created for the entire financial services industry.

Dan Sullivan: One of the things I'm fascinated with, Doug, is the unique way in which you have the advisors of each of your clients speaking the same language. I mean, this is just the opposite of what happens in the real world. That type of situation is fraught with conflict and misunderstanding. Can you talk a bit about what you've seen as a result of your TEAM members speaking the same language?
Doug Andrew: Dan, this is what I'm most passionate and excited about because it's simply about being interested in their client from a loftier perspective: their family, their virtues and values, their heritage. Then we look at their intellectual assets, their wisdom and knowledge. And, finally, we get down

to their financial and civic assets, and combine these, much like Lee Brower does in his process. The accountant, the attorney, the realtor, and the mortgage planner all come together in that commonality. Their goal is to achieve what the client has articulated is most important to them—and, believe me, it's far more than money.

Dan Sullivan: What's the before-and-after picture, Doug? What kinds of testimonials have you received?

Doug Andrew: Just to give you one example, we had two gentlemen come through a couple of years ago, and the most either had ever earned in a calendar year was about $100,000 in insurance commission. They came through our training, and then came back for two or three refresher courses, and both of them now have annual compensation well over $1 million. We've found that the average producer who comes through TEAM training will actually quadruple their income. We get them out of The Commoditization Trap and really help them undergo a meaningful transformation in their ability to provide a unique experience to clients. We teach them how to become the lead advisor, the general contractor, the quarterback for their clients. They then are able to experience the highest compensation with the least competition. The commodity sales simply follow like icing on the cake.

Dan Sullivan: Well, that's a given.

Doug Andrew: Yes it's a given. If I stand up in front of a group of mortgage professionals and say, "How many of you would like to increase your mortgage volume 40 percent without increasing the number of loans you process? How many of you would like to have a thriving mortgage business, no matter what the interest rate environment is?" Well, everybody will raise their hands, and I say, "OK, you need to get out of The Commoditization Trap." And when they see how simple it is, they're just blown away.

Dan Sullivan: This is all very exciting, Doug. Now, for the people who are going to read this interview, what kind of action steps should they take if they want to become involved with your process?

Doug Andrew: Well, the first thing they should do is visit our website at *www.missedfortune.com*. They can download or request a brochure that includes an audio CD. The next step is attending a very intensive three-day training seminar in Salt Lake City. The first night, the advisors actually watch me put on a public seminar because I think it's important for people to see how I do it, how I operate my own office. The second day, we go through a debriefing of the previous night's experience, and they just get inundated with insights. We teach them how to explain everything to clients and create plans. The third day, we go through and have them practice their own "elevator speech," which is what to say when someone asks, "What do you do?" I can't believe how many professionals have never sat down and thought about this. Finally, we take them through The Empowered Wealth System and show them how to apply those concepts. The impact is really quite dramatic on both a personal and professional level. I get thank-you notes from spouses saying, "My husband went to Salt Lake City, and I thought he was going to come back a better insurance planner or mortgage planner, but he came back a better husband." We really strive to create a

... when social security was introduced, people had a life expectancy of seven years after retirement. Now people are living 40 years after retirement, and they're looking for someone to redefine their life.

... If financial advisors can do this as a collective community of like-minded people, that accomplishment will be far greater than any level of monetary compensation can convey.

lasting transformation for participants. So tuition for the 32-hour training is $5,995, and all of this is explained on our website and in the complimentary brochure with audio CD.

Dan Sullivan: What has this done for you personally, Doug—this great adventure that has taken place over the past few years?
Doug Andrew: It has really created a tremendous amount of peace, and I'm very grateful, Dan. I receive letters from other advisors telling me about the transformations that have taken place in their clients' lives. These are people who had no hope of retiring with any kind of dignity, and my strategies have empowered them. Now they understand how to optimize their assets and plan for retirement.

Dan Sullivan: I've always said, Doug, that innovative financial advisors like you are really at the cutting-edge in terms of addressing some of the social and economic problems that have been created by the failings of social security and other govern-ment programs designed to deal with this retirement issue.
Doug Andrew: I certainly see it that way. You know, when social security was introduced, people had a life expectancy of seven years after retirement. Now people are living 40 years after retirement, and they're looking for someone to redefine their life. So I have tremendous optimism that together we can turn this world right side up and solve some of the major problems that we're going to face in the future. If financial advisors can do this as a collective community of like-minded people, that accomplishment will be far greater than any level of monetary compensation can convey. One thing I've learned, Dan, is that when you give, you receive far more back, and so you're always in debt. And I don't know if I'll ever get out of debt because the amount of gratitude and inspiration I've received from other people over the past few years has just been tremendous.

For contact details on The True Wealth Transformer, please see page 231.

IDEA 9

Giants Come Calling

"I find that most indifference and cynicism at the bureaucratic level is a result of failure and incompetence. The moment you show these people a process that actually works, they come alive with important resources."

Giants Come Calling

Big companies realize they need your solutions.

Rob Darnbrough remembers when it occurred to him that he was doing something very important in the marketplace:

"My Second Chance process enables Canadian insurance agents to get favorable underwriting in the United States. Our re-insurance market here in Canada has become so constricted that an increasing number of big cases are being rejected by insurance companies. Because I have citizenship in both countries, I was able to establish working relationships with seven companies in the U.S. This enabled me to get underwriting for agents' cases that were rejected in Canada. When I first started this arrangement, there were other people also doing cross-border business. But after a while, the American companies had enough negative experiences with these other parties that they decided to do business only with me. Only policies coming through my process would be considered. And the biggest reason, I was told, was that I had a Unique Process, where none of the others did."

There are several things that are interesting and important about Rob's experience:

• **Solving a big problem:** There are major life insurance companies in Canada. You would think they could create relationships with re-insurance companies in the U.S. to handle large policies that Canadian re-insurance companies couldn't handle. But, no, it took a single financial advisor with a Unique Process to solve a very big problem.

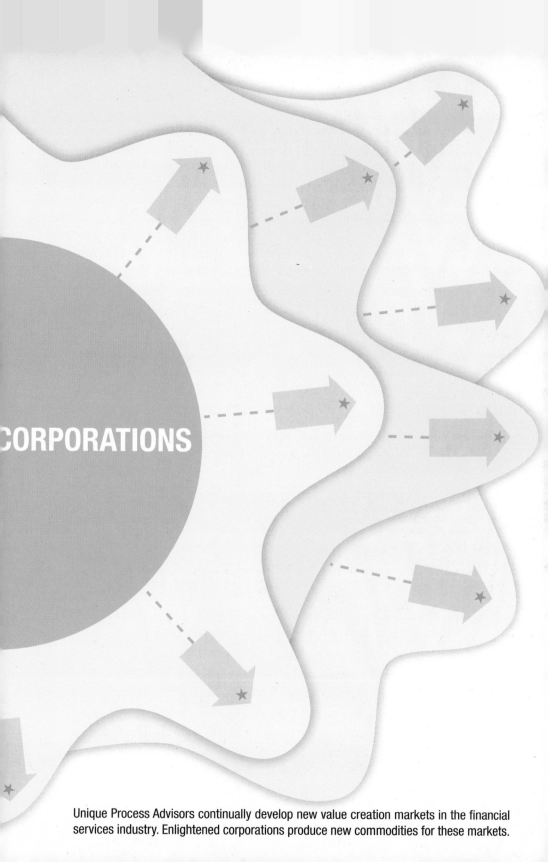

CORPORATIONS

Unique Process Advisors continually develop new value creation markets in the financial services industry. Enlightened corporations produce new commodities for these markets.

• **The process is the key:** The reason the Canadian companies couldn't solve the problem was that none of them had a Unique Process that the American companies trusted. We have discovered that, because of the mentality of head office bureaucracies, it is impossible for large companies to create Unique Processes like the one Rob has developed.

• **Saving the industry:** Rob Darnbrough told us that a significant number of top life insurance agents in Canada were thinking about leaving the industry because they couldn't place their large premium cases. His Unique Process provides them with a "second chance" in the U.S. market. Not only a second chance for their cases, but also for their careers. And in doing so, Rob is providing a second chance for the life industry in Canada, which can ill afford to continually lose its best agents.

Individuals with innovative ideas transform all industries.
The economic philosopher, Joseph Schumpeter, wrote in his book *Capitalism, Socialism and Democracy* that it is entrepreneurs, and no one else, who continually renew the capitalist system with new processes, products, and methods. This is as true in the financial services industry as in other sectors of the global economy. Unique Process Advisors like Rob Darnbrough are capable of fast, easy, and productive solutions that head office personnel cannot even comprehend, let alone create.

Mary Anne Ehlert is another prime example. With her Process For Protected Tomorrows, she is developing breakthrough solutions to problems caused by bureaucracies in at least four major industries:

"When I first began helping families with individuals with special needs, I started to run into all kinds of roadblocks. The many federal and state government agencies that were supposed to be helping these people were all failing to do so. The

educational system was dropping the ball. The housing industry and local governments were throwing up obstacles. The legal industry wasn't geared to helping them. And the medical industry, for the most part, treated them like statistics. Faced with all this, you can imagine what kind of solution a large financial bureaucracy would produce. It would take years and, in the end, produce nothing. And, yet, with our process, we were able not only to overcome all of these obstacles, but to transform all of these parties into enthusiastic partners. I find that most indifference and cynicism at the bureaucratic level is a result of failure and incompetence. The moment you show these people a process that actually works, they come alive with important resources."

Rob and Mary Anne are individual entrepreneurs who have each produced major solutions that large corporations and institutions take seriously. Two reasons for their success in this indicate why the 21st century is likely to see the increased growth of a Unique Process economy. The first has to do with profitability, the second with scaleability.

More profitable: Because each Unique Process creates a Value Creation Monopoly in the financial marketplace, the Unique Process Advisors operate businesses that are increasingly more profitable than those of product-based advisors. The profitability comes from two sources. One, Unique Process Advisors can charge continually increasing fees for the transformative value they create because they operate within a competition-free zone. No other advisor can offer the kind of in-depth problem solving and planning that they can. Clients are increasingly willing to pay whatever the Unique Process Advisors ask. And, two, at the end of the Unique Process, they sell far more product than those advisors who have nothing else to sell. These product sales are more assured, and they take far less time and effort to complete and implement.

More scaleable: All product-based advisors are closed-ended universes unto themselves. Very little of what they do can be transfered to and duplicated by other advisors. In the case of Unique Process Advisors, just the opposite is true. Any advisor who adopts a Unique Process created by one of our featured advisors will experience increased revenues and profits. For most of them, the increase will be dramatic. This means that virtually every Unique Process that uses the approach we teach in Strategic Coach represents an opportunity to transform the financial services industry in significant ways.

Big companies want to be partners.
Doug Andrew has discovered that some of the largest insurance companies, as well as one of the biggest business publishers in the U.S., want to do business with him. The reasons are obvious: His Unique Process presents new possibilities for profitability and scaleability that are far superior to anything the companies can create for themselves. Doug recounts a recent meeting with executives of a major company:

"They told me that they wanted to create special life insurance products just for the advisors who are licensed to do my process. These would not be available to anyone else. When I asked them why they wanted to do this, they told me there were three reasons. One, the quality of business they were receiving from my licensed advisors was better. Two, the cases they were receiving were larger. And, three, there were a lot more of them. They told me that my Unique Process has opened a whole new sector of the market and that they see our organization as a crucial part of their growth."

Rob Darnbrough is a Unique Process innovator who has not only transformed the capabilities and opportunities of his own business, but has provided a solution to a growing problem that was threatening many highly successful insurance agents in Canada. His story is told in the interview that follows.

Rob Darnbrough
The Second Chance Program™

In this interview, it's my pleasure to talk with Rob Darnbrough, a Unique Process Advisor from Vancouver, who has created a process that is specially designed to assist Canadian insurance advisors through the intricate process of obtaining insurance offers in the U.S. marketplace on cases declined in Canada. The Second Chance Program™ not only helps advisors retain and enhance their client relationships, as well as the relationship with the client's lawyers and accountants, it helps them recoup their investment on cases that have been declined. I think you'll find Rob's story an impressive one.

Dan Sullivan: I think I'll begin this interview, as I do most of my conversations with Unique Process Advisors, by asking you, Rob, how you got started in the industry.
Rob Darnbrough: I entered the industry 14 years ago and developed my practice along the same lines as everyone else. After about five years, I began to recognize a definite market-place danger that needed to be overcome, and that is how advisors and other centers of influence, like accountants and lawyers, work together. So at that point, I developed a process called The LifeSTEP Process™, which was designed to help accounting and legal firms integrate life insurance strategies into their estate planning work with clients. Although we had great success with The LifeSTEP Process, our firm began to notice some real challenges related to a shrinking of the rein-surance market here in Canada. In light of these challenges, we developed The Second Chance Program.

Dan Sullivan: This is in the large-case market, right?
Rob Darnbrough: Yes, that's right. And what began to happen is that while we put more and more files into underwriting, we started to get a larger percentage of our files coming back

> No one wants to hear that they're uninsurable. There's a definite sinking feeling when you're rejected in the market-place ... From [the client's lawyer's and accountant's] perspective, blame falls on the advisor, who couldn't deliver.

declined. No one wants to hear that they're uninsurable. There's a definite sinking feeling when you're rejected in the marketplace. It upsets the client and strains the relationship between the advisor and the client. But even more, it strains the advisor's relationship with the client's lawyers and accountants, who are not clear why the client has been declined. From their perspective, blame falls on the advisor, who couldn't deliver.

Dan Sullivan: So all the advisors who are in the big-case market now are basically competing for space with the reinsurance company.

Rob Darnbrough: Absolutely. And the challenge that advisors are facing is that if the reinsurance company has concerns about a particular strategy or proposal, it may express those concerns across the market. So if a proposal comes from more than one advisor, the company may already have a preconceived feeling about how that structure is put together, and decline solely on that basis.

Dan Sullivan: So they don't even look at you on an individual basis. You've been commoditized.

Rob Darnbrough: Exactly. In the Canadian marketplace, we have definitely become commoditized. I mean, you can spend 30 or 40 hours developing a structure and trying to provide value from the insurance world, but if you don't receive the end commodity, that time is never recouped.

Dan Sullivan: There seems to be a double danger. Not only are you cut off from the referral networks of individual clients, you are potentially cut off from the marketing networks of law firms and accounting firms.

Rob Darnbrough: Absolutely. Right now in the Canadian marketplace, it takes an average of 12 weeks from when the client takes the medical to when he or she gets an answer or a decline. So three months go by, at which time an offer might come back as negative. And the accountants and lawyers are looking at this process saying, "Do we even want to bother with this relationship and expose our client to the potential risk?"

Dan Sullivan: So this was the situation you faced when you began to come up with your innovation.

Rob Darnbrough: Yes. We had a couple of serious challenges. One was the long-term growth of our current practice, which depends heavily on our ability to provide value to the accounting and legal firms through good advice and competent underwriting. In 2003, we lost $6 million in commissionable earnings in the underwriting market through declines. Clients had engaged us to implement a strategy, had gone through their underwriting, and then, unfortunately, were declined. This had a significant and immediate financial impact. But it also began to rupture our relationships with the accounting and legal firms.

Dan Sullivan: Rob, just to get some perspective on this, if you take these same cases and move them back to when there were six or seven reinsurers, would they have been approved?

Rob Darnbrough: I have no doubt, yes. Not 100 percent, but we would probably be close to an 80 percent approval rate. We do some pre-qualifying for our clients before we even take them to medical, and up until 2003, when the marketplace shrank, our pre-qualifying gave us an 80 percent success rate.

Dan Sullivan: So while you increased in skill, the playing field you were operating on was deteriorating.

Rob Darnbrough: Exactly. And these challenges were ultimately what motivated us to develop The Second Chance Program and enter the U.S. market. As we assessed the situation, we began to ask whether the U.S. market was facing the same issues. We realized that while some of these challenges were being felt to a lesser degree, the U.S. market still had nine reinsurers. These firms had a far greater ability to compete against one another for offers and spread their risk. As you know, the U.S. market is ten times larger than the Canadian market, which allows reinsurers to be far more competitive when making offers. So having been born there, I decided to become licensed in the United States. Once I became licensed, we began to test some of those files that had cost us $6 million in revenue when they were declined in Canada. To our surprise, we weren't only getting insurance offers on these files, we were actually getting offers at standard rates. And we were able to recover $4.8 million of the revenue lost in 2003.

> ... the real impact was that we were now able to deliver the value we had promised to the client. We became a solution provider in a situation that was potentially very negative ... It was like having the oxygen turned back on.

Dan Sullivan: And you got the relationships back.

Rob Darnbrough: Yes. Of course, the revenue helps, but the real impact was that we were now able to deliver the value we had promised to the client. And those relationships in the accounting and legal world that had been ruptured were repaired. We became a solution provider in a situation that was potentially very negative.

Dan Sullivan: It must have been a remarkable couple of weeks after this happened to you.

Rob Darnbrough: It was like having the oxygen turned back on. We were able to overcome a situation where all our hard work and value creation was being squandered due to a shrinking market.

Dan Sullivan: I suspect the fact that you now had this extraordinary capability that couldn't be matched by anyone else in the Canadian marketplace became part of your upfront discussion with clients and also with legal firms and accountants.

> ... I quickly realized that these challenges were hardly unique to our company ... We saw a real opportunity to create value, not only for our clients, but for other advisors, who could in turn use this structure to create value for their clients.

Rob Darnbrough: That's right. Today, not only do we have the ability to go to the U.S., we have expanded our knowledge base and resources in this area. We're able to deal with cross-border tax plan issues and other issues related to buying a policy in the United States for a Canadian client. And our process provides a structure for addressing all the questions clients and their advisors might have.

Dan Sullivan: Now, I want you to talk a little about your decision to market this process to other advisors in Canada. Why did you go in that direction?

Rob Darnbrough: Well, I quickly realized that these challenges were hardly unique to our company. They were being felt across the marketplace. So the opportunity to make a significant impact was clear. We saw many advisors throughout Canada who needed something to help them recoup their investments on cases that had been declined. They needed to retain and enhance client relationships and grow their revenue. We saw a real opportunity to create value not only for our clients, but for other advisors, who could in turn use this structure to create value for their clients. And you know, Dan, we never saw these initiatives as a threat to our core business because as we learned in Coach2, one by-product of value creation is that your competitors become your clients.

Dan Sullivan: Rob, could you give us some insight on how the carriers south of the border are looking at this, because I would think it might appear new and unusual to them?
Rob Darnbrough: Well, at the beginning, they were very excited. And then some things were done by others in the marketplace that made them a little nervous about how this was being handled and whether it was being regulated correctly. So they actually closed new contracts from Canada in 2005. But we were fortunately able to retain our relationships.

Dan Sullivan: What kind of confidence level were you able to provide to them?
Rob Darnbrough: We increased their confidence by taking them through our process and our systems of delivery. We made it clear that we had taken a lot of steps and explored all the legal issues and tax planning issues. I think it gave them a tremendous amount of confidence to see the amount of work we had put into developing the process.

Dan Sullivan: This touches upon an experience common to all our Unique Process Advisors. When you can show you're operating from a process standpoint rather than just a transactional standpoint, they're much more interested in cooperation.
Rob Darnbrough: That was certainly the case in our experience.

Dan Sullivan: Why don't you take a minute, Rob, to detail the various stages of your process?
Rob Darnbrough: Sure. The process, as you know, is called The Second Chance Program, and it has six steps that we work through. The first step is The Opportunity Session™, an introductory session to make sure that the advisor is comfortable working with Second Chance and we're comfortable working with them. We discuss how The Second Chance Program can be integrated within their office and how we can work together on the files. The second step is The Preliminary

Identifier™. Here, we begin to confront situations where files are getting declined or heavily rated. We try and get information back from the advisors to understand how they're working the marketplace and what kinds of ideas and strategies they're pursuing. Then we move into a level of greater specificity with The Underwriting Assessment Filter™. Here, we begin to assess the actual situation at hand. What are the health issues? What tests have been done by the client? Once we get that information, we will contact the advisor within 48 hours and let him know whether or not it's a worthwhile endeavor for us to take the file into the United States. If it's worthwhile, we'll provide the advisor with the information and paperwork that needs to be signed by his client and begin the process of transferring the underwriting file to U.S. carriers.

Dan Sullivan: Then you actually start your dealings with the carriers.

Rob Darnbrough: Yes. At this advanced stage of the process, The Negotiated Advantage™, we begin negotiating with the carriers. As far as I know, we are the only non-U.S.-based company able to do that. We work through all the major carriers. Then if we do get an offer back, we begin The Implementation Facilitator™, where we assist the advisor with the implementation of the strategy. We work with them on all the issues involved with bringing a policy back into Canada. The last stage, The Policy Monitor™, involves the monitoring and maintenance of the insurance policy. We send out an annual report, along with a quarterly statement, that keeps the advisors informed of what their clients' policies are doing. We also offer a full-access 1-800 number where they can get any information they need to answer their clients' questions.

Dan Sullivan: So throughout the process, you really provide a lot of Back Stage support services.

Rob Darnbrough: Definitely. For example, we provide advisors with access to a secure website where they can obtain pertinent marketplace information. If they have a client who has been declined, this information can help them decide whether it's worthwhile to fill out the additional paperwork and go into the United States. We also provide them with a number of success stories to help them communicate this information to clients, along with literature and marketing material.

Dan Sullivan: Rob, what has been the response from your own clients?

Rob Darnbrough: Well, when we show them that there is a potential lifeline to go into the United States, they're encouraged. But, of course, they don't want to go through any further medical testing. So when we assure them that all they have to do is fill out a couple of forms, they're very interested. One case I like telling people about involves a stockbroker who is quite successful. He has some significant capital gains tax liability. This individual has a passion for hunting, and that leads him to Africa each year for big game hunting. The Canadian insurers were concerned about the countries he was traveling to and declined to make an offer on those grounds. When we went into the United States, not only were the insurers comfortable with the travel, they gave us the amount of coverage we needed. We were able to set up some private foundations and additional planning opportunities for the client.

Dan Sullivan: Do you generally find an improvement in the actual value of the structure when you go south of the border?

Rob Darnbrough: Absolutely. On average, we improve the value proposition by 25 percent. Now, of course, if we can procure an offer in Canada, we'll go with that because it's usually in the client's best interest to take an offer here. But if we're forced to go into the United States, we've found that 92 percent of cases have had successful results.

Dan Sullivan: Wow, that's really impressive. What has been the response of the carriers in Canada?

Rob Darnbrough: Well, in the beginning, there was some concern that we were going into the U.S. and taking business away from the Canadian market. We explained to them that our first objective is to try and place coverage in Canada. Both the insurers and advisors realize that the market here in Canada has shrunk. And I think the carriers understand our position and our need to provide value for clients. After all, we're only talking about business they aren't interested in taking. It's not a real loss for the insurers in Canada because they have the first opportunity to take that business.

> What Second Chance does is allow you to deliver results for your advisors that you may not have been able to deliver previously. So we're creating that value for the managing general agents, and many of them have already started to work with us.

Dan Sullivan: It would seem to me that it's actually in their best interest to support you because they don't want to disrupt their relations with the advisors.
Rob Darnbrough: That's a great point, Dan, but the value proposition extends beyond the insurer to the managing general agents, who have traditionally provided value to insurers through their ability to negotiate offers. With these changes in the marketplace, the value being offered by the managing general agents is being reduced. What Second Chance does is allow you to deliver results for your advisors that you may not have been able to deliver previously. We're creating that value for the managing general agents, and many of them have already started to work with us.

Dan Sullivan: Rob, what are the conditions of your own remuneration in these dealings with other advisors?
Rob Darnbrough: It's pretty straightforward. We simply take a managing general agent's override and provide advisors with

all the compensation in the file—basically a straight MGA relationship.

Dan Sullivan: Just from working with you in Coach2, I know that you are a very creative person. Do you see any further dimensions to The Second Chance Program?
Rob Darnbrough: There are a number of by-products that we're working on developing around The Second Chance Program, and we've had discussions about moving into other countries, such as Australia. So I think there is some opportunity because the process is sound. There are some different legal restraints and challenges in each country, but they can be overcome with the right process.

Dan Sullivan: You also have expansion plans throughout Canada, right?
Rob Darnbrough: Yes. We're in Vancouver, and we've opened new offices in Calgary and Toronto. In five years, we plan to have an office in all the major cities, each one with a CA, CLU, and two administrative people. Our growth has really been exponential since we introduced the process.

Dan Sullivan: What has been the response from your staff?
Rob Darnbrough: It's been fantastic. As a firm, we get together off site for two days every quarter to work on strategies for developing and improving the process. My staff has the confidence to work through issues and overcome pretty much any challenges we face in the marketplace. And having such a comprehensive process gives the staff a tremendous amount of confidence and clarity.

Dan Sullivan: Before we conclude, could you just give us a few anecdotes from situations where you've successfully handled cases for other advisors, and really been a hero to those advisors?
Rob Darnbrough: There was someone we worked with in Ontario. I first met him at a conference, and he looked quite

disheveled. He was exhausted. He was working with sixty-five - and seventy-five-year-olds and continually getting declined to the point where he was considering leaving the business. His basic attitude toward his lifelong career was that it was over. We explained The Second Chance Program to him and walked him through the process. Since then, we've implemented eight files that were declined and recovered a million dollars in commissions for him. So he's had a complete turnaround both in his business and his mindset.

Dan Sullivan: Our whole attitude at Strategic Coach is that if you have a unique capability, you try and share that capability with as many other people as possible. But I've known many financial advisors over the years who, when they have an advantage like yours, a secret market, won't tell anyone else about it. So I really want to compliment you on the expansiveness of your thinking and the expansiveness of your spirit in becoming a facilitator for so many other people.

Rob Darnbrough: Thank you. I appreciate that, Dan. You know, I can't emphasize enough how powerful it has been for our company to learn how to enter into conversations that are process-driven and D.O.S.-driven. We have the confidence that if we take a file and create a solution, the only reason a client wouldn't go forward is that they didn't understand the benefits clearly enough. That's how confident we are in the value proposition we're building, and it's an incredible feeling moving forward.

For contact details on The Second Chance Program, please see page 231.

IDEA 10

Making Everything Better

"That's when I had this idea that making things better for millions of people was a good way to stay excited and motivated for the rest of my life—and to make a lot of money."

Idea 10

Making Everything Better

Bypassing bureaucracy to transform society.

Charlie Epstein remembers how a single thought transformed his career direction, purpose, and meaning:

"I got into financial services because it gave me a better living than being a starving actor. That was it. I needed to make a good living. Even as my income continued to grow, something was missing with regard to making a contribution that went beyond making a good living. It was only after I had transformed my 401(k) practice into a Unique Process that it occurred to me that, through sharing this solution and the systems I had created for myself with other advisors, I could make an exponential and transformational impact on the entire retirement savings industry. Advisors in the industry even say, 'I can't believe you're sharing this with me!' The way I see it, this collaboration has allowed me to play an active role in helping to solve America's savings problem, assist the American worker to achieve their Desirement™ dreams, and helped me to stay excited and motivated in my life and in my practice."

The four-stage evolution: Charlie's discovery of a greater career purpose is shared by all Unique Process Advisors. Each of the advisors in this book has experienced the same four-stage evolution as a financial advisor. The first stage is utilizing financial products and resources to create an above-average personal income. Stage two is being frustrated by the restrictions and limitations of being a product-based advisor in an increasingly commoditized industry. Stage three is creating a Unique Process to escape from commoditization. *And stage four is the*

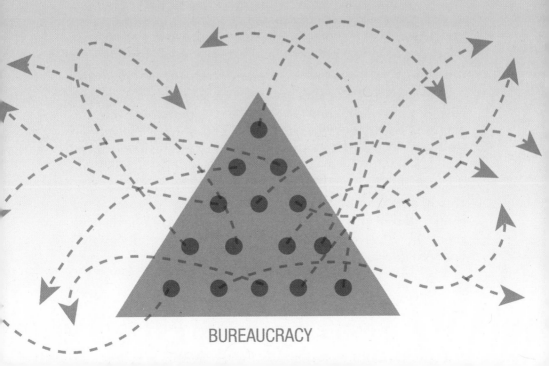

discovery that in creating greater freedom and opportunity for themselves, they have also created a plan and a path that provides extraordinary value for many other people.

Complexity is the problem.

In helping many other people, the Unique Process Advisors all tell a similar story about what gave rise to their motivation. Tom Miller explains:

"I began to notice that the products we were using for solutions weren't addressing the problems of complexity that the clients were facing. It occurred to me that I was trying to do brain surgery with a hammer and screwdriver. Financial products as they are provided by the companies are blunt instruments that don't address or satisfy the subtle and sophisticated issues that clients have. When I first designed The VisionLink Solution, it was to compensate for the deficiencies of the products. Then, it quickly dawned on me that it wasn't the fault of the products. The main deficiency was in my whole approach to the complex reality of clients' businesses and lives. As soon as I began to approach everyone using a process that put their issues and aspirations at the center, and forgot about the products, everything started to work. I became more valuable and more successful. And, in the end, the products actually became more useful, but only as tools."

Intellectual technologies that produce simplicity: The 401k Coach and The VisonLink Solution are intellectual technologies for continually transforming clients' complexity into simplicity. Charlie Epstein and Tom Miller have developed processes that enable them to use their wisdom and creativity to deal directly and effectively with the issues that overwhelm the thinking and undermine the confidence of their clientele. This is also true of all the other Unique Processes that are spotlighted in this book. They all transform complexity into simplicity in ways that cannot be achieved by product-based financial advisors—or any other kind of advisors.

In working with hundreds of financial advisors with Unique Processes, I have identified four areas of extraordinary value creation that have resulted from their work:

- **Simplicity of information.** In our 24/7 electronic age, information overload is an increasing burden for many people. Every Unique Process provides a filter that enables clients to identify only that information that is crucial for their increased sense of direction, confidence, and capability. *No financial product can provide this filter, but every Unique Process does.*

- **Simplicity of choice.** More information creates more choice. But when people have too many options, they can become paralyzed. Every Unique Process provides a systematic path to make the best possible decisions on an ongoing basis, and also provides a custom-designed gameplan for transforming those decisions into the most effective actions. *No financial product can provide this gameplan, but every Unique Process does.*

- **Simplicity of time.** For most people today, time is the scarcest resource in their lives. We all face demands on our time from a growing number of sources. Every Unique Process provides dramatic short cuts in people's time management of their work and their lives. Because the process always revolves around each individual's deepest values and greatest aspirations, the clients gain a great sense of integration in crucial areas of their lives. *No financial product can provide this integration, but every Unique Process does.*

- **Simplicity of finances.** A bewildering menu of financial products and services is presented to individuals, most of them provided by large, impersonal institutions. Few people have skilled, personal, long-term advisors. Every Unique Process provides a uniquely personalized support system that continually enables clients to eliminate their dangers, capture their opportunities, and maximize their strengths over the course of a lifetime. *No financial product provides this support, but every Unique Process does.*

Transforming complexities in every area of life.
When I talk about these four areas of simplicity, everybody I've ever met voices enthusiastic interest. These filters, gameplans, integrations, and supports are what most people are missing in their present lives, and what everyone wants more of in their future. As Charlie Epstein puts it, helping to provide these "life benefits" to large numbers of people is intensely and permanently motivating. As Tom Miller learned, it is these benefits that people most value and appreciate. The nature of our electronically-connected world is that every area of human life is taking on greater complexity. This will always be the case. Each individual increasingly needs better filters, a gameplan, continual integration, and a support system that is custom-designed for him or her. Financial advisors are in a favored position to provide these benefits in a marketplace without limits. But they can't do it by basing their businesses on products that are increasingly commoditized. They can only do it by creating Unique Processes that connect their packaged wisdom and creativity with the specific issues and aspirations of each client or customer.

Freedom: As their ranks grow, Unique Process Advisors will not only be transforming the financial services industry, but also other industries, and a growing number of social and political fields. Since Mary Anne Ehlert is an example of a Unique Process Advisor who is already having this kind of societal impact, I leave the final words in this section to her:

"You begin to realize that you have a freedom of thinking and action that others don't. With The Process For Protected Tomorrows, I'm able to create solutions for families that are impossible to create within any of the large institutions and

organizations. Our work is already widely admired throughout the country in many different sectors. We are seen as innovative and integrative problem solvers in a field where so many dedicated people are bogged down in bureaucracy and red tape."

Betty Norman's whole philosophy in life is to make everything better in the lives of her clients. Her Unique Process enables her to do this in a highly satisfying way. In the following interview, let's look at how Betty creates exceptional value for her clients in a way that a product-based advisor could never accomplish.

Betty Norman
Life Perspective™ Financial Planning

Elizabeth (Betty) G. Norman, CFP®, a long-time Strategic Coach client, is one of Southern California's leading planners and a top producer in the financial services industry. She is the founder of Life Perspective™ Financial Planning, an innovative consulting program that enables financial planners to create deeper, more productive relationships with their clients by strategically integrating their life goals and financial objectives. A former professor and counselor, Betty has developed a unique perspective related to financial planning. She has conducted over 200 financial planning seminars and has communicated her wisdom internationally. I know you'll enjoy hearing Betty's story and her insights.

Dan Sullivan: In this book, we talk with ten advisors at the cutting edge of the industry. I think it's appropriate that we conclude by highlighting an advisor who really does personify where I think the trajectory of this profession is going. Betty provides a powerful example of a holistic approach to advising that places the client's own life plan—his or her goals and aspirations for a richer, fuller life—at the center of the financial planning process. So, to begin our conversation, Betty, why don't you tell us how you started in the industry?

Betty Norman: Well, Dan, I've been in the financial services industry for over 20 years. Before that, I was a college professor and a counselor at a university. A key moment in my professional life, however, was when I had the realization that clients are just as interested in their life pursuits and the direction of their lives as they are in their money and financial health. So I began to recognize that there's more to advising than just restating a client's financial planning objectives and resources.

The key moment in my professional life was when I had the realization that clients are just as interested in their life pursuits and the direction of their lives as they are in their money and financial health.

Dan Sullivan: Betty, how long did it take before this became obvious to you?

Betty Norman: It probably became obvious sometime in the last 12 years. It was only over the last seven years, however, when I started to develop a process, that I could accommodate this request of clients. In the past, if I were to have these conversations with clients, it would take up a significant amount of time and essentially function as a value-added.

Dan Sullivan: That's the case with many advisors who are paid purely on commission. They can't afford to give any kind of in-depth service because they are simply not being paid for it, and time doing that is time taken away from their chances of actually getting paid on a commission basis.

Betty Norman: Absolutely.

Dan Sullivan: Of course you don't have to worry about that problem anymore, Betty, because you've developed a Unique Process. So why don't you walk us through the process?

Betty Norman: Our process is called Life Perspective Financial Planning, and it incorporates five interrelated stages. Through our life-centric planning process, we are essentially aligning the clients' most meaningful life pursuits, whatever they are, with their financial objectives and resources. The first stage is The Life Perspective Assessment Process™, and this is where we use our vision and discovery tools to help clients get a clearer understanding of their goals and objectives for the future. Then we move into our second stage, which is The Financial Perspective Expander™. Here, we strictly zero in on the clients' finances. We are guiding clients to a deeper understanding of their financial strengths and capabilities.

We keep them focused on their finances.

Then we move them to The Life Perspective Expander™ phase. This is where clients have an opportunity to explore their most meaningful life pursuits. They can really start formulating goals and objectives in the context of their financial situation. That leads to the fourth stage, The Life Perspective Solution™, which is critical because we take all the knowledge from the previous stages and begin to create solutions that encompass both life decisions and financial decisions. The final stage we call The Life Perspective Realization Phase™. This stage involves our ongoing efforts to implement solutions and deal with the changes that invariably come about as clients themselves change. Our process is very adaptable and flexible because we've found that, as clients begin to gain more confidence, their vision becomes clearer.

Dan Sullivan: I can imagine there is a lot of going back and making things more precise and adding dimensions as you go through this.
Betty Norman: That's exactly what happens. So, Dan, this is the process we take them through, and as we enter our sixth year, I'm happy to say that every one of my original clients is still with me.

Dan Sullivan: That's just phenomenal, Betty.
Betty Norman: What I'm noticing is that my clients are much happier. They come in on a regular basis. I don't even have to call and confirm their appointments. They joke that I know more about them than their own children do.

Dan Sullivan: Now, Betty, when I've brought up the subject of life planning—because I've told a number of advisors that you have this process—they all say, "Well, we do that too. Any financial planner does life planning." Could you differentiate what you mean by life planning from how it's usually considered by financial advisors?

Betty Norman: Well, Dan, most financial advisors see life planning as asking their clients to give them ten goals. What would they like to accomplish? And the goals are really rather general, and they're not related to what we consider the clients' most meaningful life pursuits. What we do is get down to the very core of what these individuals want and what they would like to transfer to their spouses, to their children, and to their grandchildren. We've designed tools that ask the right questions in a way that they don't feel like you're intruding on their privacy. These tools are getting to what, really, life planning is all about and how it's related to their finances.

Dan Sullivan: What is the general profile of the clients you work with?
Betty Norman: Well, this process works well with everybody. Everyone has these concerns: "Will I retire successfully? Will I achieve my life goals?" People want to align their values and life pursuits with their financial objectives, but they also want to know how they can transfer their values to significant others.

Dan Sullivan: Betty, I understand that you've been expanding this idea of transferring core values to the next generation and beyond. Can you talk about that?
Betty Norman: Dan, we've been developing and working with a model called Value It→Live It→Transfer It™ that expands the idea of legacy planning to include the transfer of personal values like tradition, culture, charity, education, work ethic, or any other value important to clients—rather than just the transfer of wealth. We realized that you can't dictate values in a will or trust document. If you want someone to adopt your values, it has to be done through experiencing and internalizing those values now. In essence, you end up with a two-part legacy plan: One part deals with the division of your assets when you die, and the other deals with transferring your values now. We support this using custom-designed tools based on the Value It→Live It→Transfer It™ model to work with our clients.

You know, Dan, I really do believe that the baby boomers are going to rewrite retirement. They are intently focused on enjoying life now, while also passing on those meaningful life pursuits to their family.

> Most important, I have been able to reduce my client load. At this stage in my life, I'm not really interested in having 1,000 clients. So right now, 50 people are basically paying for my business.

I always say, Dan, if you are a good financial planner, you're going to handle your clients financially; otherwise, they wouldn't be with you. That's why as financial planners, we need to offer clients a wider, more meaningful experience, while always staying focused on the financial fundamentals.

Dan Sullivan: What has the effect of working with your clients in this way been on your own professional life?
Betty Norman: Our business is growing by leaps and bounds. We have increased our revenue from fees by at least 40 percent. Most important, I have been able to reduce my client load. At this stage in my life, I'm not really interested in having 1,000 clients. So right now, 50 people are basically paying for my business. I'm obviously doing a better job with each client, and when I look at the appointment book, I look forward to seeing who's coming in.

Dan Sullivan: Well, in the past, you were giving away those services rather than charging for them as part of a process. How has client appreciation changed now that clients are writing a check?
Betty Norman: It does make a difference. In general, the clients are so pleased with what they're getting that they never even question writing the check. As you indicated, I did formerly give away that advice as a value-added. I'm going to spend time with my clients and talk about their life goals

whether or not I'm getting paid—that's just my professional inclination. So now that I'm getting paid, it does remove a lot of the previous frustrations.

Dan Sullivan: What about referrals?
Betty Norman: That's an interesting question, Dan, because I used to never understand why I wasn't getting referrals. I approached some clients and asked them directly, "I've been good to you. You enjoy coming here. So why aren't you giving me referrals?" I was shocked when they said, "Well, we don't want you to get too busy."

Dan Sullivan: Your clients were probably very perceptive. They were concerned about you being misused. And I think your clients were actually zeroing in on the fact that they appreciated enormously that you were giving them something very precious, but they also realized that you weren't necessarily getting paid for it. So I think they were probably trying to protect you.
Betty Norman: That's a great point, Dan. Now, of course, clients are paying me, and as I said, I've been able to reduce my client load and really focus on providing an exceptional experience to a core group of clients—from whom I am now getting referrals.

Dan Sullivan: And you have also reduced your marketing costs.
Betty Norman: I don't even market. I don't do seminars anymore. I don't need to struggle for referrals as if my business depended on them. I'm able to pick and choose.

Dan Sullivan: You also don't need to push product and rely on product sales.
Betty Norman: Absolutely. I'm going to get paid regardless of the products I'm selling, and the clients actually appreciate that because they know it ensures independence. The result is that clients who may have their money scattered with other people are eager to put it all under my management. Even

though I'm only seeing 50 clients on a quarterly basis, the money they're bringing in is astronomical.

Dan Sullivan: I would also suspect, Betty, that not only have you added another 40 percent on top of product, the actual money you are receiving from product has also increased.
Betty Norman: Right. Our trails have increased. We're only selling those products that are best for the clients, but the numbers are well above previous levels, and that's considering we're working with fewer clients.

Dan Sullivan: What kind of fee structure are you operating with?
Betty Norman: We have various levels, and the fee structure is primarily based on what we need to do. So we have a range of around $4,000 to $12,000 in annual fees, which are paid in quarterly installments.

Dan Sullivan: Talk a little about the team and organizational structure you have developed around this process.
Betty Norman: Well, I have great back-office support. My oldest son is a financial advisor with an MBA. My daughter is a professor with a PhD from Stanford who helps out in the office. In general, the team we have now considers this more than a job, and they are really gratified by the relationships being developed with clients.

Dan Sullivan: I know that a lot of advisors are concerned about succession issues. And it seems that not only do you have a supportive family involved, you have a process that can go on within your own structure.
Betty Norman: That's right, Dan. It could go on with my son. It could go on with any of the financial planners we bring in. What we've done is developed a turnkey program, and it goes from A to Z. Every tool comes with examples and supporting commentary.

Dan Sullivan: That gets to my next question, Betty. Like all of our other Unique Process Advisors, you've made efforts to package this turnkey process for other advisors in the profession. Why don't you talk about those efforts? When did it occur to you that you might want to package this for other advisors?
Betty Norman: Well, it started occurring in the Strategic Coach Program, when I had an opportunity to talk to some of the Unique Process Advisors who have had success along these lines. I came back from the meeting and said to my son, "You know, we have a product that is just as effective. We can do this. It's a natural fit." From there, we set the wheels in motion, and it has been a continual effort at fine-tuning.

Dan Sullivan: How many advisors are currently involved?
Betty Norman: We have about 25. We have two broker-dealers that are on board and will allow their planners to use the process. We just presented to a very large insurance company, and they're quite receptive. As I said, there is still some fine-tuning, but we're getting close to being able to really roll this out on a larger level.

Dan Sullivan: What kind of investment is required in terms of time and resources from advisors who want to become involved?
Betty Norman: Well, right now we have a one-and-a-half-day workshop. Our goal is to increase the clarity and confidence of the planners regarding our process and make sure they understand exactly what we are trying to accomplish—the mindset that is required to succeed with this approach. We have software and a book that will be available on Amazon.com by late summer 2008. It's called *The Life-Money Connection: What Most Financial Plans Miss And How To Add It*. It's written for the general public and is designed to support advisors in explaining our process to their clients. In terms of financial investment, certainly our workshop carries a fee. Advisors often try out different seminars, and some have had bad experiences in other places. They come to us and say,

"You know, I've paid out thousands of dollars to other programs that didn't make a difference. But with you, after a matter of months, I made $50,000."

Dan Sullivan: That must be very satisfying, Betty.
Betty Norman: You know, Dan, at this stage in my life, I've made enough to retire, and I wouldn't be trying to push something if I didn't think it was extremely beneficial and transformational for those involved.

Dan Sullivan: As we wrap up this interview, Betty, I want to talk about a problem that is certainly facing the financial services industry right now, and that's the problem of legal risks. As you know, the charges for errors and omissions and other compliance issues are going through the roof. And it seems that with a single solution, you've solved an enormous number of legal issues, because I can't imagine a situation developing where one of your clients would want to sue you.
Betty Norman: You are absolutely right, and the reason is because we have a process in place for finding out what the client wants. Everybody is on the same page. Clients walk in, we have a meeting, and then we send a follow-up report. There is no lapse of memory. We've had two broker-dealers give their blessing to this process because they recognize that it is the epitome of the most important command in the industry: "Know your client."

Dan Sullivan: And you are, by and large, insulated from fluctuations in the market.
Betty Norman: Dan, I honestly believe that if their portfolios produced five percent, the clients would be happy. I mean, five percent is not very good, but the clients are so thrilled to see how their financial objectives are aligned with their life objectives, that that synergy is worth everything to them.

Dan Sullivan: I've been talking about this, Betty, since the early

1990s. I feel that financial advisors in the 21st century have a unique role to play in American society and other developed countries. More than any other professional in the market-place—lawyers, accountants, psychologists, even clergy—financial advisors are in a position to have meaningful conversations about their clients' goals and life objectives. As a result, financial planning will increasingly emerge as the single most influential advisory profession in the marketplace. And I think your process really sits at the forefront of these trends.

Betty Norman: That's a wonderful insight, Dan, and I do believe that we as financial planners have an opportunity to pull all of these strands together and gain that centrality in the lives of clients.

> I truly believe that if advisors would add the experience element, the life-centric approach, then they could start developing a different relationship with clients.

Dan Sullivan: Clients need the kind of support that you and other innovative financial planners are providing, especially with the decline of so many other institutions and sources of support in American life. I mean, the traditional model of life-time employment and stable retirement that come with work in a large corporation is largely outdated. It strikes me that really great financial advisors who are life-centric in their approach can respond to the needs of hundreds of thousands of people who want a sense of direction and confidence and capability in their lives.

Betty Norman: Absolutely. Talking with my colleagues, everybody is concerned about their business and the pressures and so forth. I truly believe that if advisors would add the experience element, the life-centric approach, then they could start developing a different relationship with clients.

Dan Sullivan: Betty, if we were having this discussion ten years from now, what would you have liked to see happen with this process as it goes out into the marketplace?

Betty Norman: Well, I would hope that we will have had the opportunity to present this across the nation. I really see this process as a new model for financial planning that can reshape the profession if enough people adopt it. As I talk with you today, Dan, I'm more energized than ever and ready to see that transformation through.

For contact details on Life Perspective Financial Planning, please see page 233.

VISION

Unique Process Significance

For the first time since financial services became a distinct industry, the process of marketplace innovation has shifted from large corporations to thousands of individual entrepreneurs. This trend will accelerate as more advisors adopt the Unique Process model as the dynamic foundation of their businesses and careers.

Unique Process Significance

Transforming every aspect of financial services.

The Unique Process Advisors featured in this book are harbingers of a major direction that financial services will take during the 21st century, at least in advanced societies like the United States, Canada, Australia, and the U.K. As more consumers grow wealthier and more individualistic in their aspirations, they demand more specific transformations of their specific dangers, opportunities, and strengths. Corporations cannot meet this demand, but Unique Process Advisors can and will. As we have seen, they are already doing so. The Unique Process model that we have described in these pages can be adapted and mastered by any client-focused advisor who seeks greater entrepreneurial freedom and career satisfaction.

Profound impact. As the numbers of Unique Process Advisors reach into the thousands, their combined innovations in the marketplace will have a profound impact on the financial services industry. As we have seen from examples like Mary Anne Ehlert's Process For Protected Tomorrows, these Unique Processes also transform the structures of other industries.

For the first time since financial services became a distinct industry, the process of marketplace innovation has shifted from large corporations to thousands of individual entrepreneurs. This trend will accelerate as more advisors adopt the Unique Process model as the dynamic foundation of their businesses and careers. Many of their Unique Process innovations will direct how successful corporations will reorganize and redirect their own approaches to the marketplace.

Eight economic advantages of Unique Process Advisors.
In their relationships with large organizations, Unique Process Advisors have at least eight economic advantages that bureaucratic corporations, by their very nature, cannot match:

- **Focused Unique Ability of the advisor and their growing team:** The small size of Unique Process organizations permits a continual focusing of unique talents to produce much greater productivity in specific situations than is possible in a bureaucratic structure. Large organizations are better at producing large general results over longer periods of time. Unique Process organizations are much better at producing superior specific results in short time frames. Rob Darnbrough's Second Chance process works so well because he can deal with each insurance agent and case immediately, productively, and profitably. Rob and his team are uniquely good at this and have a passion for producing extraordinary results for each agent. No large insurance company is capable of doing this.

- **Deep, committed relationships with individual clients:** This is something that is only possible on a personal and entrepreneurial basis. Betty Norman's process, Life Perspective Financial Planning, entails a multi-year relationship between advisor and client that continually deepens the commitment, respect, and admiration on both sides. Betty's own skill and passion for this kind of relationship, and for this kind of counseling-coaching approach, bring a depth and breadth of conversational discoveries that are impossible within a product-focused sales track designed by head office managers or trainers. Large organizations can only treat individual customers as impersonal categories and statistics. Their only interest in individuals is as consumers.

- **Continually evolving mastery of clients' D.O.S. issues:** Each client's emerging issues are of immediate creative and economic interest to a Unique Process Advisor. Lee Brower's

Empowered Wealth System enables each family to create their own unique foundation for the future, based on the use of all the specific Core, Experience, Contribution, and Financial capital of all its members. Every single danger, opportunity, and strength of every member of each family is crucial raw material for creating an overall solution that will last through generations for decades. It is highly likely that the hundreds of family solutions that come from Lee's Unique Process will last longer than the lifespan of many financial corporations. For a corporation, only large numbers of consumers in the aggregate are of interest. No CEO or corporate executive team can possibly understand and respond to the D.O.S. issues of individual families the way that Lee Brower and his team are able to do.

- **Rapid response time with new value creation:** Unique Process Advisors and their teams can identify a problem one day and deliver a creative solution the next. Within his Donor Motivation Program, Scott Keffer is able to innovate solutions within a single day-long process. Scott's clients, especially on the donor side, frequently have small amounts of time and attention to devote to their charitable giving. The charities are frequently offered only narrow windows of opportunity in which to secure a donor's interest. It's essential that the problem-solving and strategic-planning process be done as quickly as possible. Corporations, conversely, take months and years to respond to general problems.

- **Low-cost research and development:** The nature of the Unique Process model is that research and development are built into its daily implementation. Unique Processes are designed for continual, never-ending trial, error, improvement, and breakthroughs. Within Debra Schatzki's Financial Services In A Box, she and her colleagues are able to test new ideas and improve their value creation approaches on a daily basis. Since the entire foundation of her Unique

Process is collaborative for everyone involved, improvements to the system and methodology are a normal, expected outcome from each meeting between advisors, accountants, and their mutual clientele. In contrast, corporations, because of their hierarchical, political, and career-focused cultures, tend to become resistant to experimentation and innovation over time.

- **Rapid profitability on innovations:** An innovation generated within a Unique Process can turn a profit within months, sometimes within weeks. Dan Taylor took his Parent Care Solution from initial idea to finished product within three months. He paid for all of his expenses three months later. Within the first year, the process was turning a healthy profit. For corporations, return on investment usually takes years from the time an innovation is conceived.

- **Low-cost, sophisticated packaging:** Unique Process Advisors take advantage of the low-cost packaging breakthroughs offered by today's ·digital technologies. Sophisticated presentations can be produced inexpensively in a matter of weeks, sometimes days. Doug Andrew finds that he is now able to develop major new presentations of his True Wealth Transformer process, including multimedia, print packages, and software tools, within three months' time. These presentations can attract the participation of hundreds of professionals in the financial, legal, accounting, and real estate industries. Doug has also created a publishing system that enables him to turn out a new best-selling book in as little as six months. All this packaging is accomplished with very little cost, utilizing the skills of a small team. Corporations, especially in financial services, labor over their packaging for months, with dozens of individuals adding to costs, delaying implementation, and often decreasing its effectiveness.

- **Successful scalability without significant capital:** Many Unique

Process Advisors are packaging their innovative models for the use of hundreds of other financial advisors. This is usually done through licensing agreements that entail an initial training program plus annual updates. These Unique Process networks can be grown with very little investment capital. They become profitable with as few as a dozen licensees. Charlie Epstein, Mary Anne Ehlert, Tom Miller, and Doug Andrew have all created major specialist networks based on their Unique Processes. They have done this with modest upfront investments of capital, and have financed their continued growth out of cash flow, accomplishing significant marketplace impact using their own resources. Financial corporations, by way of comparison, must invest millions of dollars and large numbers of manhours to make their new products and services scalable. It can take years for these initiatives to be profitable.

The ten Unique Process Advisors featured in this book are representative of hundreds of others who are developing their value creation approaches in the Strategic Coach Program. Each of these financial advisors is more profitable because of their Unique Process than they ever were as a product-based salesperson. All of their businesses are scalable to a degree that depends only on the ambition of the advisor. But whether they become major forces in the marketplace or remain simply very profitable individual businesses is beside the point. The real payoff of the Unique Process model is that each of these advisors has achieved a freedom of operation, purpose, and ambition that they couldn't have imagined when their business was based on selling commodities and limited by bureaucratic and regulatory controls. Although they spend little time reflecting on their impact on the financial services industry, it's clear that their successes are providing direction, confidence, and capability for many others. Unique Process Advisors, as role models for achieving freedom and prosperity from a base within the financial services industry, are here to stay.

Glossary

The Ceiling of Complexity™. All growth in a company occurs in stages. With each stage, and the complexity that it brings, a point is reached where growth becomes impossible with the existing knowledge, skills, and capabilities. Working harder and longer in the existing stage no longer works; in fact, it is counterproductive. This point is called The Ceiling of Complexity. To break through this Ceiling, different strategies are needed to achieve a new state of simplicity in thinking, communicating, and performing.

Coach2®. An advanced level within the Strategic Coach Program, in which entrepreneurs continually transform their companies on the basis of the accelerating development and distribution of intellectual capital. Entrepreneurs at this level all have developed Unique Processes they are charging for in the marketplace. As a result, they increase their competitive advantage within their industry and are seen as the dominant innovator.

The Commoditization Trap. The global forces of technology and deregulation have put tremendous price pressure on every product and service. More and more, clients and customers are making buying decisions based on price alone. This reduces all products and services to the commodity level. If you're doing business today, falling into this Commoditization Trap, where everything you do is judged on price, is an ever-present reality.

D.O.S.™ D.O.S. is an acronym for Dangers (D), Opportunities (O), and Strengths (S). By focusing on these three areas, it is possible to transform any prospect, client, or other important relationship by helping the other person eliminate their dangers, capture their opportunities, and maximize their strengths in order to reach their goals.

The D.O.S. Conversation®. This is a simple and highly effective way to quickly establish a relationship based on value creation. It gives you the crucial information you need to determine if and how you can provide direction, confidence, and capability to a prospect, client, or other key relationship. By focusing on the other person's dangers, opportunities, and strengths (D.O.S.), you create immediate value, clearly differentiate yourself from the competition, and revolutionize the way you develop long-term relationships with your clients and customers.

The Front Stage/Back Stage Model™. This model draws a parallel between the theater and the experience you create for your clients in your business. The goal is to create a truly unique experience in which clients see the "magic" of the Front Stage without seeing the Back Stage logistics. Everything you do on your Front Stage creates value for your clients, and everything Back Stage has a direct link to your Front Stage. The Back Stage is about creating better and better support systems that expand the impact of the Front Stage.

Industry Transformer™. As Unique Process Advisors grow their revenues and profits, and as the positive reputation of their uniquely valuable problem solving spreads throughout the marketplace, they increasingly transform the structures, relationships, and institutions of their industry. Gradually, a new industry begins to emerge as more clients gravitate to the Unique Process Advisor's new way of doing business.

The Strategy Circle®. A problem-solving and planning tool for producing dramatic results. When presented with a goal, the brain naturally responds with obstacles that oppose this vision. The Strategy Circle uses this information to create the strategies necessary to achieve the goal.

Unique Ability®. A central concept of the Strategic Coach Program, Unique Ability® is the essence of what you love to do and do best. These are a few characteristics of Unique Ability®: It's a superior skill that others value; you love using it; it is energizing both to you and to others; and there is never-ending improvement. People who identify their Unique Ability® have an extraordinary competitive advantage in any situation—but especially among those who are entrepreneurs. In Strategic Coach, entrepreneurs learn how to focus on just their Unique Ability® activities and delegate everything else.

Contact Information

Doug Andrew • *The True Wealth Transformer*™

Paramount Financial Services, Inc.
6340 South 3000 East, Suite 280
Salt Lake City, UT 84121

Tel. 1.888.987.5665 (toll free)

Email TEAMinfo@MissedFortune.com
Website *www.missedfortune.com*

Lee Brower • *The Empowered Wealth System*™

Quadrant Living Experience, LLC
801 North 500 West, Suite 200
Bountiful, UT 84010

Tel. 1.801.397.3300

Website *www.quadrantliving.com*

Rob Darnbrough • *The Second Chance Program*™

The Second Chance Program
700 West Pender Street, Suite 915
Vancouver, BC V6C 1G8

Tel. 604.630.0327 or 1.866.568.4055 (toll free)

Website *www.thesecondchanceprogram.net*

Mary Anne Ehlert • *The Process For Protected Tomorrows*™

Protected Tomorrows, Inc.
103 Schelter Road
Lincolnshire, IL 60069

Tel. 847.522.8086

Website *www.protectedtomorrows.com*

Charlie Epstein • *The 401k Coach® Program*

The 401k Coach® Program

Tel. 877.932.6236

Email info@The401kCoach.com
Website *www.The401kCoach.com*

Scott Keffer • *The Donor Motivation Program*™

Wealth Transfer Solutions
2535 Washington Road, Suite 1120
Pittsburgh, PA 15241

Tel. 1.412.854.7860

Email info@dmp-thekey.com

Tom Miller • *The VisionLink Solution*™

The VisionLink Advisory Group
7700 Irvine Center Drive, Suite 930
Irvine, CA 92618

Tel. 1.888.703.0080 or 949.852.2288

Website *www.vladvisors.com*

Betty Norman • *Life Perspective™ Financial Planning*

Life Perspective Solutions, LLC
P.O. Box 9665
Brea, CA 92822
Tel. 1.888.985.5737 (toll free)

Email info@lifeperspectivesolutions.com
Website *www.lifeperspectivesolutions.com*

Debra Schatzki • *Financial Services In A Box™ by BPP Wealth Inc.*

Weiser Capital Management
135 West 50th Street, 14th Floor
New York, NY 10020

Tel. 212.375.6582

Email dschatzki@weisercapital.com

Dan Taylor • *The Parent Care Solution™*

Advisor Freedom
3924 Cambridge Hill Lane
Charlotte, NC 28270

Tel. 704.814.9965

Email info@parentcaresolution.com
Website *www.parentcaresolution.com*

Strategic Coach

Dan Sullivan is known throughout the world as an innovator and visionary whose ideas have set the standard for others in the entrepreneurial coaching industry. The Strategic Coach Program, co-founded in 1989 with his wife and partner, Babs Smith, was the first coaching program exclusively for entrepreneurs, and remains the most innovative in terms of its ability to help participants make successive quantum leaps toward increasingly greater personal and professional goals.

Strategic Coach clients today not only significantly increase their income and free time, they build strong, future-focused companies that leave their competition behind. Many have set new standards in their industries and made significant contributions to their communities through the increased focus, resources, and creativity gained by participating in the Program. Because of these results in all areas of life, most participants continue year after year. They comment that, as their dreams grow, the Program grows with them.

On the following page is a graphic overview of the progression of the Strategic Coach Program. For each progression, a description of the key concepts, is provided. These concepts, designed to build on one another, provide continued resources and support in achieving both business and personal goals.

The Strategic Coach Inc.
Strategic Coach is an organization created by entrepreneurs, for entrepreneurs. The company operates using the same philosophy, tools, and concepts taught in the Strategic Coach Program, and has grown more than ten times in the past eight

INDUSTRY TRANSFORMER™

An innovative and autonomous entrepreneur who, operating entirely within a self-evolving Unique Process™, continually generates new intellectual capital that provides extraordinary value for clients and customers in ways that increasingly bypass and escape from the forces of commoditization, competition, and bureaucratic control.

THE LARGEST CHEQUE™

The ability to increase the size of cheques and other strategic results you achieve — thereby raising your personal confidence and organizational capabilities.

THE UNIQUE PROCESS™

The ability to package your problem-solving wisdom and capabilities into an integrated, repeatable process that makes you immune to competition and commoditization.

UNIQUE ABILITY® TEAMWORK

The ability to focus increasingly on your own Unique Ability®, surrounded by a team where everybody else is able to do the same.

Strategic Coach

The Largest Cheque

The Unique Process

Unique Ability Teamwork

Industry Transformer

Value Creation Monopoly

The Three Sales

The Bigger Future

Coach2

Strategic Coach Masters

VALUE CREATION MONOPOLY

The ability to create a unique, positive experience for clientele that permanently secures their enthusiastic, exclusive, and increasing commitment, engagement, and support.

THE THREE SALES

The ability to simplify your entrepreneurial time, effort, and focus into just three integrated abilities and activities: money, freedom, and capability sales.

THE BIGGER FUTURE™

The ability to plan and actualize a two-stage, 20-year game-plan, leading to a quantum leap in capabilities, ambitions, and results.

years. With over 100 entrepreneurially-minded team members and three offices—one in Toronto, one in Chicago, and one in the U.K.—the company continues to grow and enrich its offerings to an expanding global client base. Currently, over 3,000 successful and highly motivated entrepreneurs from over 60 industries and a dozen countries attend Strategic Coach workshops on a quarterly basis.

If you would like more information about Strategic Coach, its programs for entrepreneurs at all levels of success, or its many products for entrepreneurial thinkers, please call **416.531.7399** or **1.800.387.3206**. Or visit *www.strategiccoach.com*.

Creative Destruction

A subscription series for further reading.

Building on the concept of Creative Destruction® presented in this book, the *Creative Destruction* subscription series provides an in-depth look at several industries being affected by this phenomenon. In each module, in addition to the interviews with the Unique Process Advisors featured here, Dan Sullivan uses his intimate knowledge of the financial services industry to outline a gameplan for the future to help financial advisors reach unlimited prosperity.

As an advisor, you may be feeling the squeeze of industry change. There's outside pressure from clients and customers, who have more alternatives to choose from than ever before. Inside your industry, there's increased pressure from a growing number of compliance rules and regulations.

All of this is symptomatic of Creative Destruction, a natural force in the marketplace that has now come to bear on the financial services industry. This force eliminates old bureaucratic businesses that, in their obsession with self-interest and self-protection, have ceased to create sufficient value, and clears the way for new, more responsive organizations committed to innovation and contribution. As an entrepreneur, you have an opportunity to create a business like this, evolving faster than large organizations can, and inventing valuable new solutions that sidestep industry obstacles and create more value for your clients and customers.

In this subscription series, Dan Sullivan turns this powerful economic concept into an active process—one that you can use to transform your business. In each module, Dan expands on his bold predictions for the financial services industry and shows how you, like a group of profiled "Industry Transformers," can escape destructive market forces and become more successful than ever. In addition, you will find powerful examinations of other industries also experiencing the forces of commoditization, such as the music industry, auto industry, and airline industry. Each of these examples of Creative Destruction contains lessons that every other industry can benefit from. Finally, Dan will outline a plan and path to becoming a Unique Process Advisor.

If you would like more information about, or would like to order, *Creative Destruction*, please call **416.531.7399** or **1.800.387.3206**. Or visit *www.strategiccoach.com*.

Creative Destruction, each
USD $65   CAD $65   GBP £45.50

Creative Destruction, Modules 1-4
USD $285   CAD $235   GBP £164.50

Creative Destruction, Modules 5-8
USD $235   CAD $235   GBP £164.50

Creative Destruction, Modules 9-12
USD $285   CAD $235   GBP £164.50

Creative Destruction, Module 13
USD $65   CAD $65   GBP £45.50

Acknowledgements

A project like this always takes a talented team of people working toward the same goal: to produce a well-designed book that reads like a dream and whose message resonates with and inspires the reader. In this, I am very fortunate. I take my hat off to my team and to their admirable abilities, none of which I possess.

Thank you to Gordon Arlen, who always does a remarkable job of editing transcripts of phone interviews to fashion the interviews with our featured entrepreneurs.

To our brilliant graphic designers, Suzanne Noga and Marilyn Luff, who approach each book with a fresh eye and great enthusiasm, thank you.

Many thanks to a terrific team of editors, Catherine Nomura, Myrna Nemirsky, and Kerri Morrison, who read version upon version of the book until it finally meets their impeccable standards.

Many thanks to production manager Christine Nishino, who makes decisions on every detail of the printing of the book and coordinates with our incredible print broker, Moragh Cameron. They are both superb at what they do. And to project manager Paul Hamilton, who always manages to make the entire process run smoothly and who always makes us laugh—even under pressure.

And, finally, to our ten Unique Process Advisors, my deep appreciation for believing in the concepts and ideas we offer at Strategic Coach, and for making them work for you and the thousands of other human beings who experience your wisdom through your Unique Processes. You're all an inspiration.